From Fright to Might:

Overcoming the Fear of Public Speaking

Ron Reel
Phillip Maynard
Kenneth Klawitter
Carolyn Inmon
Liesel Reinhart
Jeff Archibald

Introduction

Table of Contents

An Introduction to Communication

This is where I start to have fun. -Lara Croft, *Tomb Raider*

ICON KEY

- Valuable information
- Activity
- See Another Chapter

His name was Corax and he came from a part of ancient Greece known as Syracuse. In the 5th century B. C., Corax published the first book designed to educate students in the art of public speaking. Skill in oratory, or public speaking, was considered essential in ancient Greece as well as many non-Western cultures. West African history, for example, has been remembered and recorded for centuries in the speeches of a *Griot*, or public storyteller. The vast oral traditions of the Winnebago, Lakota, and other Native American tribes, attest to the power and richness of live performance as a means of sharing information and teaching values.

You are now part of that history. For many of you, this class marks your first venture into the field of communication studies: an academic discipline that examines the way human beings use words, body language, and countless other forms of symbolic expression. Perhaps this is the first time you will receive training in a specific type of communication called public speaking. As you begin, realize that public speaking is only one form of communication. Scholars also examine the way we communicate in one-on-one interactions, how we communicate in our rituals and performances, how we transmit messages in businesses and other institutions, and the many ways we are affected by mass media like television and the Internet. Communication is a huge part of our lives, but what exactly does the word mean?

Communication Defined

Think about how often we use forms of the word *communication* in everyday conversation:

We just don't communicate anymore!

Let's keep the lines of communication open.

Communicate with your kids about drugs.

Even though we like to use the word, rarely do we consider what it means. The word *communication* has been interpreted and defined in literally hundreds of different ways. Here is one way to define the term:

Communication: An interactive process of sharing symbols in order to construct meaning.

This definition brings up many important issues. First, consider the idea of interactivity. Communication is often compared to a transaction in which someone gives something (like a speech) and gets something in return (nods of approval, applause, a blank stare, etc.). Communication is also a process—which means that it is ongoing or continuous. In fact, there is an old saying in the communication field that when you are in proximity to another person, you cannot *not* communicate. Next, communication requires the sharing of symbols. A **symbol** is anything that stands for something else. Words, pictures, gestures, even clothing all have symbolic meaning and, therefore, can communicate. Finally, we put these symbols together to form messages that allow us to make sense of the world around us and construct meaning.

Based on this definition, consider whether or not the following scenarios are examples of **communication**:

- **A young woman yells at her boyfriend. He says nothing, turns around, and walks way.**
- **Stella walks into class wearing her Air Force uniform.**
- **You are lost in the desert. You build a fire and send smoke signals for help.**
- **A father sings to his baby until she falls asleep.**
- **Samantha, the family Doberman Pinscher, barks and whines until her owner lets her outside.**

- **A young child carries on an imaginary conversation with a teddy bear.**

- **A woman walks alone on the beach, reminiscing about her youth.**

As these examples suggest, determining what constitutes communication can be tricky. One way to get a clearer grasp on the concept is to consider the elements present in the **communication process.**

One of the most vital elements in the communication process is the **sender** of a message, known in public speaking as the **speaker**. This is the person or people responsible for creating and/or transmitting a **message**. The message is the content of the communication, both verbal and nonverbal.

Elements in the Communication Process:

- Sender (Speaker)
- Message
- Receiver (Listener)
- Feedback
- Interference
- Medium (Channel)
- Context

The **receiver** (or listener) is the person, or, often in speech, *people*, for whom the message is intended. When receivers respond to a message, it is called **feedback**. During a speech this feedback can be verbal or nonverbal.

Sometimes messages are altered or obstructed in the communication process because of **interference**: factors that get in the way of or change the intended message.

The **medium** is the channel used to convey a message. For instance, when you watch a televised sporting event, the medium is television.

Finally, communication does not exist in a vacuum. The time of day, location, previous events, and other variables all shape the communication act. **Context** is the term for the environment in which communication occurs.

Public Communication Goals & Benefits

People speak in public for a variety of reasons: to teach a lesson, to sell products, to commemorate an occasion, to inspire an audience, and to remember a loved one. Even though there are many reasons for giving speeches, most can be categorized as having one of three primary goals: **to inform, to persuade,** or **to entertain.**

Certain speeches are designed to fulfill one of these overall goals. For example, a classroom speech discussing how to create a web page is primarily a speech to inform. On the other hand, a speech that uses humor to convince listeners to exercise regularly is designed primarily to persuade but may also entertain. Understanding your primary goal is helpful when preparing a speech. In speaking, as in life, clear goals lead to more successful outcomes.

Goals of Public Speaking:

- To inform
- To persuade
- To entertain

Speaking of goals, what are your goals for this class? Many of you may be here simply because your school requires this course for graduation. That is a pretty good reason, but it is not the only benefit to be gained from studying and practicing public speaking. There are also academic, career, and personal benefits.

ACADEMIC BENEFITS

Public speaking is not the only class where you will be asked to deliver a speech. Many instructors require oral presentations in courses as diverse as art history, French, or even physics. Your instructors know that if a student has the ability to explain material orally, he or she truly understands the information. Be sure to apply all that you learn in this course when given speaking assignments in other classes. All of your presentations should be logically organized, supported with relevant research and content, and delivered in a clear and engaging style.

When choosing a major and/or minor, you may wish to consider speech communication as a field of study. Many attorneys, counselors, entertainers, and businesspeople major in communication before pursuing specialized training.

Also, if you want additional experience with public speaking, consider joining a club or organization that offers performance opportunities. Toastmasters International has more than 8,500 clubs in 70 different countries. Group members gather to perform speeches and hone their communication skills. You can find a local organization at www.toastmasters.org. Your college likely has many groups that also offer speaking opportunities such as student government, mock trial, drama, and forensics—another name for competitive speech and debate.

CAREER BENEFITS

Unless you win the lotto or retreat to the wilderness to hunt and fish for your survival, one day you will enter the work force (if you have not already). No matter what your employment, chances are that effective communication skills will be vital to success in your career.

Jobs in Communication:

- Speechwriter
- Journalist
- Mediation Specialist
- Non-Profit Director
- Political Analyst
- Press Secretary
- Media Critic
- Television Reporter
- Trainer
- Lobbyist
- Motivational Speaker
- Sales Representative
- Diversity Consultant
- Public Relations Coordinator
- Speech Instructor
- Sports Promoter
- Many others

Most members of professional organizations, from CEOs to entry and mid-level employees, are expected to speak both within organizations and to the public. In fact, according to Julia Wood in her 1998 book *Communication Mosaics*, during any given 24 hour period during the workweek professionals will deliver more than 30 million presentations. The November 1st, 2001 issue of *Career World* cites a report from the National Association of Colleges and Employers that claims "the top 10 qualities employers seek have little to do with technical skills and a lot to do with personality and attitude. Employers want team players with great verbal and written communication skills."

Even if you enter a profession in which you will not be expected to deliver speeches or interact with the public (which is highly unlikely), everyone must interview for a job. The skills you acquire in this course as well as other communication courses can help you land a job and succeed once you are hired.

Avg person spent 30% of his waking hours in conversation.

PERSONAL BENEFITS

Finally, public speaking can provide the personal benefits of improving your overall knowledge and confidence. Putting together an effective speech makes use of a variety of critical thinking skills including researching, organizing, analyzing an audience, and writing. Expect these skills to improve as you progress through the course. You will also gain valuable knowledge about the topics you cover in your speeches and the topics covered in your classmates' speeches. All in all, this class is a fantastic opportunity to improve skills and gain knowledge about a number of compelling issues and topics.

Public speaking can also improve your confidence. As discussed in the next chapter, most of us have anxiety about speaking in public. Learning to control that anxiety will make you a more confident speaker and will also build self-esteem that may help you overcome other obstacles in your life.

Becoming an effective speaker will also help you become a more dynamic member of your community. We live in a democratic society that depends on truly informed and active citizens. Whether you're running for political office or just speaking up at a city council or school board meeting, the power of public speaking will help you shape and direct the community in which you live.

While effective speaking skills can result in a number of benefits, with these benefits also come some responsibilities. Chief among these responsibilities is the obligation to make sound ethical decisions.

Ethical Considerations

Ethical decisions are those that try to answer questions of right and wrong, good and bad. Sound ethical choices are crucial for communicators since public speaking can be such a powerful tool. When he was president, Teddy Roosevelt coined the term "bully pulpit" to describe the powerful position that public speakers enjoy when they voice views and opinions. Why are speeches so potentially powerful? In a speech, the verbal communication of information is primarily one-way. The speaker's opinions, for the time being, are the only ones being voiced.

Also, the charisma or presence of a dynamic speaker can be a persuasive force that causes audiences to rely less on their critical thinking skills. The persuasive charisma of Adolph Hitler, for example, is a well-documented and sobering reminder of our responsibility to make ethical decisions regarding the integrity of our information and the sensitivity we demonstrate toward our audiences. Let's consider three overall ethical considerations: integrity of information, speaker sensitivity, and listener etiquette.

INTEGRITY OF INFORMATION

Speakers are ultimately responsible for the reliability and accuracy of the information they present. Here are two common ways in which speakers lose their integrity when delivering speeches.

Plagiarism

The single biggest threat to your integrity is the academic crime known as plagiarism. If you take someone else's words or ideas and pass them off as your own, then you have committed plagiarism. The problem has reached epidemic proportions on college campuses across America. According to *The Chronicle of Higher Education*, February 15, 2002, over 25% of students admit to plagiarizing written assignments like papers or speech outlines.

Students can plagiarize in several ways. First, if you use someone else's entire speech or find one on the web and then present it as your own, you have committed **comprehensive** plagiarism. If, however, you point and click your way through journals, magazines, or newspapers and copy sections to incorporate into your speech, you have committed **cut-and-paste** plagiarism. Finally, if you pay or convince someone else to create an entire speech on your topic, you have committed **customized** plagiarism.

Comprehensive - using someone's speech

Cut & paste - use 2-3 diff. speeches to make one

Customised - have someone to do it.

Regardless of the method, plagiarism is harmful to individuals and to society. In the moment, plagiarism may seem like a quick way to make your life easier. However, reading, writing, and thinking skills are ultimately neglected when we cheat. These skills are exactly what employers are looking for in potential employees. We also damage the whole educational process when we cheat. Consider, for a moment, a future workforce of doctors, engineers, nurses, teachers, and airline pilots who bluffed their way through college by passing off someone else's words or ideas as their own.

Also realize, if you do plagiarize, there is a good chance you will get caught. More and more instructors are employing sophisticated anti-plagiarism software that checks written work against a large database of books, magazines, newspapers, and journals. The price for cheating may range from a failing grade on that assignment to more severe punishments including withdrawal from the course or even expulsion

Imci - using little part of someone speech's in your speech without giving credit.

Do yourself a favor. Never plagiarize. Trust your own ability to think and create. Always make sure that the work you submit is your own. If you would like to use other people's words or ideas, you may—*as long as you credit the original source in your speech.* Giving credit to sources keeps you from plagiarizing and, at the same time, builds your credibility. No one expects you to be an absolute authority on each of your speech topics.

☆ First Amendment gives us the freedom of Speech.

Information Accuracy

In addition to creating all your own work, be sure that all the work you create is honest and accurate. Below are some ethical misdeeds that students commit when creating speeches.

Lying

Creating imaginary sources or changing the information you uncover is obviously wrong. After all, the point of using research in a speech is to uncover the truth. Also, if you uncover information that directly contradicts your point, you cannot ignore it.

Manipulating or exaggerating research

Although rounding off complicated numbers or statistics is fine, never manipulate your research to the point where it could be misinterpreted. For example, a college president might brag that her school has seen a 300% increase in Native American student enrollment. If, in truth, the number of Native American students has increased from one to four, these numbers do not live up to the magnitude that was implied in the president's comments. You, as the speaker, have the responsibility to determine the most legitimate way to present your statistical information.

Using outdated information

Your audience is relying on you to present the most current information available. In fields such as computer technology, medical science, and business, for example, changes occur at a rapid pace. Depending on your topic, information that comes from sources only a few months old may already be out of date. Your ethical obligation is to be up-to-date on your subject so that you do not unintentionally mislead or misinform your audience.

SPEAKER SENSITIVITY

In addition to having information integrity, you must also be sensitive to your audience. Your audiences will be comprised of people from different ethnic, cultural, and socioeconomic backgrounds. Also, differences in age, religion, sexuality, work experience, and other variables mean that each of us has a different life experience. We see the world in different ways. When you deliver a speech, you are speaking to a diverse audience that may or may not hold the same beliefs, attitudes, or values that you do.

Effective speakers are sensitive to the diversity of their audience and adapt their speeches to ensure they do not isolate or offend a group of people. Sensitive speakers never *intentionally* use racist remarks to offend audiences. Also, sometimes we *unintentionally* isolate groups of people when we assume that everyone shares the same religion or comes from a household that earns a certain amount of money.

Being sensitive to diversity *does not* mean that you must always omit information with which people may disagree. If you only tell audience members what you think they want to hear, you have failed to be an ethical speaker, too. Stand up for your beliefs. Just make sure to respect the differences that exist in today's world and be open to potential criticism of your message.

LISTENER ETIQUETTE

Listeners also have an ethical responsibility in the speech making process. At the basic level, audience members should be *courteous*. Here are some simple tips for being a polite audience member during classroom speeches:

1. **Sit up straight, and do not slouch or move around.**
2. **Clear your desk of distracting material.**
3. **Turn off all cell phones, pagers, and/or beepers.**
4. **Never talk to a classmate while someone is speaking.**
5. **Never walk into or leave a room during a speech.**
6. **Avoid coughing, eating, or getting into your backpack during a speech.**
7. **Maintain eye contact with the speaker for the entirety of his or her speech.**

In addition to being courteous, you can also go a step further and become a *supportive* audience member by following these guidelines:

1. **Smile at the speaker during his or her speech.**
2. **Nod your head when the speaker makes a particularly good point.**
3. **Laugh when the speaker attempts to use humor.**
4. **Applaud when the speaker is finished.**
5. **Encourage others around you to be as courteous and supportive as possible.**

In Chapter 4 of this textbook we will discuss listening in greater detail, but as a final note on the ethics of listening, consider whether or not you will remain silent after hearing a presentation. At the end of each speech given in your class there may be an opportunity to discuss the speech, speaker, and topic. You might want to praise the speaker for a speech you thought was particularly noteworthy. Likewise, you have a right to voice criticism or dissent as long as you do so in a respectful and courteous manner. Silence is often taken as acceptance. If you are quiet because you disagree with the message of a speech, a potential discussion on the subject may not take place. Your silence may shut down opportunities for the meaningful exchange of ideas that is vital to any course.

Conclusion

In this chapter, we have introduced the concept of communication—a concept as old as recorded history. We have also looked at the importance of public speaking both to our society and to its citizens. We have considered the goals of public speaking as well as the ethical obligations of both speakers and audience members. This is just the beginning.

From FRIGHT to MIGHT Moment

As your first speech approaches, there is a strong likelihood that you are feeling a little apprehensive or nervous. Take a moment to talk to some of your new classmates and you may discover that you have a very sympathetic audience for your first speech.

Speakers' Secret

Remember that while speaker sensitivity is important, you should not be afraid to voice unpopular opinions.

As long as you are polite and respectful, voicing dissent is not only "ok" but vital to the success of a democracy.

Chapter 1: Terms & Concepts

Bully Pulpit
Communication
Comprehensive
Cut-and-Paste
Customized Plagiarism
Context
Feedback
Group
Information Accuracy
Interference
Listener Etiquette
Medium
Message
Public Speaking
Receiver
Speaker Sensitivity
Sender
Symbol
Statistical Manipulation

Works Cited

Wood, Julia. *Communication Mosaics.* Wadsworth, 1998: 372.

Kellogg, Alex P. "Students Plagiarize Online Less Than Many Think, a New Study Finds." *The Chronicle of Higher Education* 15 Feb. 2002: 44.

Wallis, T.J. "Skills Every Employer Wants." *Career World* 1 Nov. 2001: 15.

ACTIVITY #1: Understanding Chapter 1

Answer the following items as true or false.
Answers appear in Appendix C.

1. It is unlikely that other classes in college will require oral presentations.	T	F
2. Most scholars agree about the definition of communication.	T	F
3. There are four major goals of public speaking.	T	F
4. Buying a paper on the Internet and turning it in as your own is known as "cut-and-paste plagiarism."	T	F
5. The alteration of messages during the communication process is known as *interference*.	T	F

ACTIVITY #3: Introducing Someone Else

Interview a classmate. Use some of the following questions and some of your own to find out more about the person. Then write a short (under one minute) speech to introduce this person as a guest speaker for a class or other event. Your introduction should make the audience feel excited about the person you introduce!

Some Questions to Ask:

What is your ancestry/heritage?

Where were you born?

Are you named after someone?

What is your major?

What do you plan on doing in 10 years?

What do you like to create?

What sports or music do you like?

Do you like to keep physically fit?

Do you have any children?

What is your favorite TV Show?

What is your favorite movie?

What are three adjectives to describe yourself?

Write out your introduction here:

ACTIVITY #4: Communication Scavenger Hunt

Although people generally associate communication with words, an important concept in this unit is that almost anything can have communicative value. Form teams and go outside of your classroom to collect one item for each category listed below. **You may not use any items in your classroom or that you brought with you to class today.** After you have located the items, put together a group presentation about the objects you found. All group members must participate in the presentation!

1. Something that communicates love
2. Something that communicates evil
3. Something that makes an argument
4. Something that has the goal *to inform*
5. Something that has the goal *to persuade*
6. Something that has the goal *to entertain*
7. Something that is representative of your group
8. Something mentioned in a song (Your group must perform at least 10 seconds of the appropriate part of the song).

Additional Rules:

- Time limit = _____
- No splitting up, and learn each other's names!
- No breaking of laws or school policies.
- All valuable items must be returned after class.
- No repeat use items.
- Be creative!

Speech Anxiety

Aaron: *You better practice your speech.*
Jane: *I can't. I get scared just thinking about it.- Broadcast News*

Speech Anxiety is sometimes also called *Communication Apprehension, Stage Fright*, or even *Butterflies.*

Adrenaline - butterfly, in stomach

Madonna feels it. Jay Leno says he has experienced it. Barbra Streisand is said to have it so severely that she can barely perform for live audiences and must have every word of her lyrics on Teleprompters in case she goes blank. Even your public speaking instructor has probably felt it many times.

Speech anxiety, or stage fright, is a very common phenomenon, but for newer speakers, it can be overwhelming.

Feelings of anxiety can show up as late as the last point of your speech or as early as the moment the speech is assigned. You may have already felt it in this class. If so, you aren't alone. Public Speaking is probably the class that students fear more than any other class.

Anxiety often takes the form of a shaking hand, pounding heart, sweaty palms, chest pain, dizziness, or butterflies in the stomach – but sometimes it can be more severe. Feeling nauseous, having to go to the bathroom, even fainting has been known to occur because of a speaking event. Psychologically, the anxiety may cause procrastination and negative self-talk before the speech, and "blanking" during the speech (not knowing what to say next or forgetting a portion of your content).

Symptoms of Speech Anxiety:

- Racing Heartbeat
- Sweating
- Nausea
- Breathing Difficulty
- Dry Mouth
- Shaking/Twitching
- Wringing of Hands
- Nervous Laugh
- Panic
- Pacing

As you prepare to speak, your brain tells your body it needs assistance to get through the task at hand. Your brain then sends communication via hormones and your nervous system to your body that will require one of two responses – fight or flight. If you fight, you're going to respond to the challenge to the best of your ability by preparing and delivering the best speech possible. If flight is your choice, you will avoid the causes of this anxiety by missing the speech, withdrawing from the course, or even dropping out of college.

Unfortunately, many students consider dropping public speaking classes or changing majors to avoid public speaking. People with speech anxiety are known to receive poorer grades in school and many of these students are more likely to drop out of college. They also cannot perform certain jobs.

Certainly public speaking is widely known as one of the top human fears. In the March, 1991 issue of the *Public Relations Journal*, Robert Edward Burns refers to a study by R.H. Bruskin which stated that, "among adults surveyed in 1973, 40.6% picked public speaking as their number one fear." He further confirms that this fear is still prevalent by referring to the 1977 *Book of Lists* which surveyed 3,000 people and identified the fact that public speaking outranks insects, bugs, and death as the greatest fear.

Things have not changed very much. In a CNN broadcast that aired March 19, 2001, a Gallop Poll is cited in which public speaking is listed as the number two fear among Americans, surpassed only by the fear of snakes. Since your instructor will probably not bring snakes to class, the fear of public speaking may be the greatest obstacle you will need to overcome in this course.

Reasons for Speech Anxiety

Speech anxiety can be caused by a number of different factors, most of which are in our control.

Often, our **lack of speaking experience** is to blame. Remember the first time you rode a bike, rode a rollercoaster, or drove on a freeway? You probably felt some anxiety. But the more times you do something, the less nervousness you will probably feel. The same is true with speaking. Most people in college have not had the opportunity to give many formal speeches in their lives. Much of the nervousness you feel may simply be from doing something unfamiliar to you.

Other factors can also enhance anxiety. Perhaps you had a **prior negative experience** in your past, such as a classmate laughing at you during a class presentation. James Earl Jones, who was tormented as a child because of his stuttering, credits public speaking for allowing him to overcome this problem. Even though there may just be one brief episode in our past, it can impact us for years to come.

Reasons for Speech Anxiety:

- Lack of speaking experience
- Prior negative experiences
- Fear of being the center of attention
- Low self-esteem
- Concern about being "judged"
- High stakes
- Feeling subordinate to the audience
- Feeling different than the audience
- Degree of unpredictability
- Self-fulfilling prophecy
- Excessive self-focus instead of audience-focus

Almost all young children want attention. However, as they grow older, things can change. They may find themselves avoiding the spotlight and experiencing the **fear of being the center of attention.** If you have speech anxiety, search your past. When was the first time you recall *not* wanting people to pay attention to you?

Low self-esteem increases anxiety. If you don't feel good about who you are, then you may not feel you have anything meaningful to share with an audience (even though you probably do). For people who are not confident about their abilities, speeches can also lead to **concern about being judged** by the audience. Often we let what *they* think about us mean more than what *we* think, even though that doesn't make much sense.

The **high stakes** of a speaking situation can make even the most confident speaker quiver. Stakes are the outcome of a speaking situation, such as a job (for a job interview), a grade (for a class speech), or an award (for a speaking contest). The higher the stakes, the more nervous we may become.

For instance, Madonna was asked to sing at the Academy Awards™ a few years ago after a song she recorded was nominated for an award. When the moment in the show arrived, she strutted onto the stage confidently with a big, white feather boa draped from hand to hand and began to sing. However, a few lines into the song, she dropped the boa from her right hand and, for a flash, the audience could see that her hand was trembling severely. In front of a billion people and desperately wanting the respect of her peers in the film industry, even the bold, brave Madonna was experiencing stage fright.

Madonna isn't the only one to be afraid when the stakes are high. Journalists, when conducting interviews, may experience butterflies. Even the highly paid and professional Barbara Walters attests to this.

Feeling subordinate to the audience implies feeling "less" than them in some way. If you had to defend yourself in front of a judge and jury, you might feel intimidated because of their positions and power. A similar concept is **feeling different than the audience.** This occurs when you realize that those individuals listening to you are not your peer group. For instance, a male speaking to an all-female audience might be more nervous than he would be speaking to a group of mostly men.

The **degree of unpredictability** can enhance anxiety. This fear of the unknown happens when you find yourself in unfamiliar circumstances. This might include being asked to speak at a moment's notice, being forced to answer a question out loud in class, or giving a speech to another speech class. This is why some people become especially nervous about giving impromptu speeches, being promoted, or changing jobs.

Some speakers act out the **self-fulfilling prophecy.** Speakers who are afraid they will fail tell themselves from the onset that there's no reason to prepare because they won't do well anyway. Because of this lack of preparation and negative attitude, they are not successful and therefore confirm in their mind their prediction of a poor performance.

Overall, though, probably the single biggest factor in speech anxiety is our **excessive self-focus**. Simply put, we spend way too much time thinking about ourselves and not enough time thinking about our audience.

In virtually every speaking situation, except possibly a job interview, the goal of the speech is to inform, persuade, or entertain the audience – not just to evaluate the speaker.

Yet, people often forget that and obsess about how they will be perceived by the audience – smart or stupid, attractive or awkward, funny or silly. Your speech is not about you; it's about your topic. You don't "speak for yourself," you speak for your audience.

There's an old wives' tale that suggests to get rid of speech anxiety, you should picture your audience naked. That's terrible advice. Instead, picture your audience dangling from a cliff, and imagine that the words of your speech are the information they need to pull themselves to safety. If you are focused on your audience and constantly obsessed with whether or not they *understand* what you are saying, you won't have a chance to worry about yourself.

It's natural to worry about how we appear to others. Remember, you present yourself to people all the time, every day. Speech is just an extension of the kind of communication you do on the phone, in person, or over the Internet. If you can push through your anxiety, you'll have the power to help, influence, and entertain your audiences more effectively.

Overcoming Speech Anxiety

There are many things you can do before delivering your speech that may reduce your anxiety. Consider some of the following techniques.

BEFORE THE SPEECH

Prepare for the speaking event. Singers don't sing in public until they know the words to their song. Speakers should not speak before an audience until they have practiced their speech enough so the audience will gain knowledge and respect for the speaker. The more you practice, the less anxiety you will experience.

Know your own strengths and weaknesses. Each public speaker has strengths and weaknesses. If you are a great storyteller, make sure to use that strength while giving a speech. By using what we know we do well, there is less to fear. Also, know your weaknesses. If you are uneasy with statistics, don't fill your speech with numbers. If numbers are needed, choose them wisely and place them where absolutely necessary. The more you know about these two areas, the better your speech will be. When you are in control, there is less to fear.

Familiarize yourself with the speech situation. The key is to control all of the elements you can. Arrive early to the room where you will be giving the speech. Walk to the front or wherever you will be speaking, and practice your speech. Examine how far away the audience will be from you while you are speaking. Adjust the lectern if needed. You will have eliminated potential fear that might have caused you to be less effective.

Get ready to speak physically and mentally. Before you give any public speech, you need to make sure you are physically and mentally ready. Make sure you get enough sleep the night before. Be cautious of additional caffeine to wake you up. Take a couple of deep breaths before you are called upon or introduced as the speaker. Many professional trainers prepare mentally as well. They call this "visualizing." This happens when you visualize yourself speaking successfully. This can be done as part of your practice. Close your eyes and visualize yourself giving the perfect speech you have constructed. Notice your delivery, the organization, and the response you want from the audience. Michelle Kwan, World Champion figure skater, claims that before every competition, she visualizes her entire program from start to finish before stepping onto the ice. This exercise will help overcome the fear that you won't be able to complete the speech -- because you have already "seen" yourself do it.

Realize your audience wants you to do well. You are very lucky. Because you are enrolled in a beginning public speaking course, all of the other students have an added reason why they want you to be successful. Each student realizes he or she will be giving speeches in front of the class. If you make a mistake, the classroom audience will be supportive of your efforts and want you to continue speaking because they are emotionally involved with you as a member of the class. There is no need to fear your class audience; they are just as afraid if not more frightened than you are.

Know that it looks worse from inside. We are our own worst critics. You are going to feel more nervous than you look. Your audience cannot see everything you feel. Because of the higher energy level we experience while speaking, we lose some perspective while speaking. A pause that is only two or three seconds in length may seem like an eternity when standing before the class. After you finish your speech, a classmate may comment on how effective the pause was in the speech. It may have been enough time for that person to catch up and understand the point you were making. Audiences tolerate a few mistakes from beginning speakers because it demonstrates they are learning the process of speech making.

Understand stress. Stress and fear are often used interchangeably in the public speaking situation. Don't forget that some fear or stress is beneficial to public speakers. When we experience stress or fear, we become energetic and become more alert. Because of this fear, our body produces more adrenaline and extra blood sugar. This in turn, gives us the extra strength needed for gesturing, projecting, and being involved in our speech. Adrenaline is the same hormone that athletes depend on – and you can make it work for you in the same way.

DURING THE SPEECH

Sometimes anxiety flares up during a speech performance. Consider the following advice to reduce your anxiety while you are speaking.

Accept that you are experiencing some level of fear. Remember that fear gives us extra energy to convert or channel into positive outcomes. Don't dwell on the fright. Acknowledge it and move on. Many speakers claim that the only time they worry about a speech is when they *don't* feel any fear.

Engage in positive self-talk. Each time a negative thought enters your head, dismiss it with positive affirmation. If you think, "I cannot do it," replace it with, "I can and will do it." Tell yourself that you have prepared properly for the speech. Affirm that your topic is worthy of sharing with your audience.

Breathe. While you are speaking, remind yourself to keep taking regular, deep breaths. Many speakers are afraid to stop talking long enough to breathe regularly – and this can create a tense feeling in the chest or even make a speaker feel faint.

Don't apologize for being nervous. If you don't tell the audience about your nerves, the audience won't be looking for it. By calling attention to the problem, you ask the audience to notice an issue that would probably go unnoticed otherwise.

Focus on the audience, not yourself. If you concentrate your energies on how the audience is reacting to your speech, you will have little time to worry about yourself. Instead of wondering if the audience likes you or thinks you are a good speaker, obsess about whether or not the audience understands your message. Many speakers feel an immediate improvement in their anxiety level if they can get past thinking about themselves and instead think about the audience.

AFTER THE SPEECH

After the speech is over, you should **evaluate yourself** to help build your confidence for future speaking situations. It is very healthy to evaluate your performance once it has been completed. This evaluation must be done in relation to where you are as a public speaker. We would not expect a beginning public speaker to evaluate his or her performance in the same manner as the national collegiate champion.

Conclusion

In this chapter we have discussed the number one fear for Americans – public speaking. We have examined the reasons for speech anxiety and how to overcome it. If, as you progress through this course, you experience anxiety, revisit this chapter for assistance in managing your fear.

From FRIGHT to MIGHT Moment

Give yourself permission to grow. Many people feel they are the same today as they were yesterday. However, a quick check will show that not to be true. Even if you feel afraid of speaking today, keep an open mind about how you might change in the next few weeks or months. You may just surprise yourself.

Speakers' Secret

Gain experience by speaking as often as possible.

Public speaking is a learned behavior. You must do it to become successful at it. Try to volunteer as a public speaker. Seek opportunities where you can give oral presentations. Every time you give a speech, you will become a better speaker. You will stop feeling afraid of public speaking and begin to look forward to the opportunity provided to you.

CHAPTER 2: Terms & Concepts

Communication apprehension
Self-fulfilling prophecy
Speech anxiety
Stress
Subordinate

ACTIVITY #1: Understanding Chapter 2

Answer the following items as true or false.
Answers appear in Appendix C.

1. Adrenaline is a hormone that increases your heart rate.	T	F
2. Lack of speaking skills may increase speech anxiety.	T	F
3. Fear will eventually go away on its own if you wait long enough.	T	F
4. People with severe speech anxiety are more likely to drop out of college.	T	F
5. Breathing can be related to feelings of anxiety.	T	F

Activity #2: Fear Confession

This activity is to be done in conjunction with the first speaking experience in front of the classroom. First, rate your anticipated fear before your first speaking experience. After your speech, rate your actual fear. Choose a partner and share these results with him or her.

1. **Rate your anticipated fear using 1 as "No Big Deal" and 10 as "I'd rather die than do this again."**

1 2 3	**4 5 6 7**	**8 9 10**
1-3	**4-7**	**8-10**
low level fear	Noticeable fear	High level fear

2. **Rate your actual fear after your speech:**

1 2 3	**4 5 6 7**	**8 9 10**
1-3	**4-7**	**8-10**
Low level fear	Noticeable fear	High level fear

3. **Share your fear with a friend, asking these questions:**

- When did you feel the fear?
- What were the physical manifestations of the fear?

Preparing and Delivering Your First Public Speech

"I'm speechless. I have no speech." - George Costanza, *Seinfeld*

Your instructor is about to assign your first public speech. Perhaps you've done some ice breakers, but now the first speech is coming up.

Have you set aside enough time to prepare your first speech for this course?

Carefully preparing the content of the speech is very important. The Boy Scout motto is, "Be prepared." It's a philosophy just as important in public speaking as it is in camping and hiking. Preparation is all the work you do prior to a speaking event to shape your content and delivery. Preparation time for a speech can be very short – one minute, 20 seconds, or even less.

Preparation can also take hours, weeks, or even months for a very important speech. Typically, the President of the United States will prepare for several weeks for the State of the Union address each January. Unfortunately, many speakers do not prepare enough for speeches, and the result is often a disappointing performance.

The importance of preparation cannot be overemphasized. There are three advantages:

1. **Preparation impacts your speech content and delivery.**

2. **Preparation impacts your credibility.**

3. **Preparation decreases your nervousness.**

An old Chinese proverb says, "The journey of a thousand miles starts with a single step." The road to becoming a great communicator never ends. There is always something to learn, but for now, you need to start somewhere. This chapter addresses the beginning steps to start you on your journey.

The Top 10 Steps to Preparing & Delivering Your First Speech

STEP 1: CARE

The first step is to **care**. It sounds so simple, but you must care when you stand up in front of the room. Your instructors see so many students who walk up to the front of the room who look like they just don't care and would rather be somewhere else. Maybe they are trying to look cool; maybe they chose a topic they don't care about. For whatever reason, they seem bored or distant.

This completely ruins a performance. An audience must invest valuable time to listen to your speech. Showing you care proves to them you appreciate the investment they are making in you. Marco Benassi, a professor at The College of DuPage in Illinois, writes in *Six Keys to Effective Public Speaking*,

"Your audience will NEVER care more than you do."

Find *something* to care about in every speech you give. If you don't care about your topic, your audience, or yourself, you can't possibly get a message across to others.

When you care, you will reflect it through the energy in your voice, the expressiveness of your face and posture, and the preparation and quality of your work. It actually smoothes over mistakes you make. If your audience knows your speech is important to you, they will want you to succeed.

STEP 2: ORGANIZE YOUR THOUGHTS

A speaker who rambles or drifts from idea to idea is difficult for an audience to follow. Every time you speak, then, try to establish a clear pattern for your thoughts. Consider your speech as a journey that requires a beginning, middle, and end.

Your classroom speeches should follow a typical pattern of **Introduction** (beginning), **Body** (middle)**,** and **Conclusion** (end)**.** Try brainstorming to discover all the interesting ideas you have. Jot down the ideas you want in the speech, and decide which ones are the best. You may then want to organize the information in your body into a couple of major groups also known as **main points.**

You will learn many more ways to organize speeches in Chapter 8. For your first speech, though, be sure to plan out each segment of your presentation. Your instructor may give you a specific structure to follow.

STEP 3: START STRONG/END STRONG

Your speech begins the moment the first audience member realizes that you are the speaker. **Approach** the front of the room with confidence and in a professional manner. Pause before you start to let the audience orient themselves to you visually. Smile. Breathe. Begin.

At the end of your speech, **exit** in a professional way. Don't run off. Hold your eye contact, then leave slowly and with confidence. Also, never end a speech by saying, "That's it" or "I'm done." Even though you hear it done a lot, avoid saying, "Thank you." The fact that it is done often makes it a cliché, a phrase that has lost its meaning from overuse. Additionally, it makes little sense to thank an audience after you have just researched, prepared, and delivered a speech for them. It is best to let a meaningful idea resonate in their minds, rather than a meaningless phrase like "Thank you."

Pay special attention to the first and last lines of your speech. Your first line grabs the audience's attention, and your last line is the impression of you they will carry with them. Know exactly what you plan to say. You may even want to memorize them so you can look directly at your audience when you say them.

Practice the end of your speech so your last line has closure. Raise your pitch and volume slightly near the end of the line, then pause slightly and drop your pitch at the end of the sentence. This is a nonverbal cue to your audience that the speech has finished, and can help avoid the awkward moment when an audience isn't sure if they should applaud or not.

STEP 4: LOOK GREAT/FEEL GREAT

Your audience will make a number of determinations about you by your **appearance**, just as you probably do when you visit an airport or mall and "people watch." If you were to stand in front of an audience silently with no expressions at all, what would your appearance communicate?

The audience sees you before they hear you. So make that first impression a positive one. Even if you can't afford fancy clothes, you can still look great for your speech. *Everyone* can afford:

- **A shower and neat hair**
- **Clean, pressed clothes**
- **A good night's sleep**

In fact, how you dress is another way in which you communicate *caring*. When you have a big date or occasion, like a wedding, you probably dress up to show others that the event is important to you. You can communicate the same thing by dressing in the best professional clothes you can afford for your speech performances.

Common Appearance Distractions:

- Loud, shiny or flashy jewelry (especially on or around the face)
- Poorly fitted clothing
- Chewing gum
- Hats, sunglasses or glasses which conceal the eyes
- Prominent fingernails
- Revealing shirts and skirts
- Clothes with logos and messages
- Being less well dressed than your audience

You can also make sure you are looking good by avoiding appearance distractions. The table to the left summarizes some common appearance problems that distract your audience from your message.

Not only is it important to look great, you should also feel great. Your physical well-being is key to a great performance. Make sure you are well-rested, have eaten, and have had plenty of water before giving your speech. You may want to bring a bottle of water with you to class. If you do, make sure to leave it at your desk when it is your turn to speak.

STEP 5: SHOW YOUR PERSONALITY

The next step is hard for some people while easy for others: show your personality. Each person has a different type of personality. Some are shy and some are outgoing. However, even people described as shy can be expressive when you get to know them. Those who are shy have to work hard to take this step in speaking style. If you don't think you have a personality type, use this opportunity to develop and define your own.

Often, because of anxiety, speakers freeze up when they get in front of an audience and speak softly or without much animation. Yet, this isn't how they talk to their friends or family. Showing your personality means that you talk to your audience with the same natural enthusiasm you show to those who are close to you.

Greg Dolph, an instructor at Mt. San Antonio College, says that we should, "make friends with our audiences." We are spending several minutes with them and we should let them get to know us a bit during that time, just like we would if we met them at a party.

The number one tool you have in your personality arsenal is your **smile**, and you must smile in front of every audience. Even if you have a bad message for them, they need to like you. Let them dislike your *message*.

Another powerful personality source is your sense of **humor.** Try to add a little humor to every performance. Audiences respond very well to humor if it is natural and stems from your personality.

STEP 6: NEVER DROP THE BALL

Just like in sports, an important rule for new speakers is to never drop the ball. Dropping the ball happens when you make a mistake while speaking, but it is not the mistake itself. A ball is "dropped" the moment that you comment on your mistake, verbally or nonverbally.

It is natural for people to stumble or even blank out occasionally, but how you handle it in the moment makes a big difference. A speaker who drops the ball may roll her eyes, make a twisted face, verbally apologize, lose her confident posture, giggle, or even walk away. A speaker who holds on to the ball will not comment on the mistake. She will simply stay "in the moment," maintaining eye contact, holding her last expression, and concentrating until she is ready to start speaking again.

When you make a mistake, it is very hard not to comment about it, but try. When you stop talking about your topic and start talking about yourself, the speech loses focus and becomes about *you*. But your speech is not about you; it's about your topic and the audience (remember this lesson from Chapter 2?). Dropping the ball also causes you to lose **credibility** – the audience's perception of your ability to be a competent and likeable speaker.

Finally, never ask, "Can I start over?" If your audience has seen you begin your speech already, there is no starting over. They can't erase the impression they already have of you. Just stay focused and pick up at the next place you remember. By the end of your speech, the audience will hardly remember the mistake.

STEP 7: CONTROL YOUR BODY

Just like problems with appearance, excessive or improper body movements can distract your audience. In fact, Debora Dragseth, a professor at Dickinson State University, wrote in the *Bismarck Tribune* of July 18, 2000 that too much fidgeting lowers the audience's confidence in you. Therefore it is essential that you work to control some basic physical elements.

When a speaker's legs are shifting, wiggling, leaning, and even wandering around the room without purpose, the effect is all the same: it brings the attention of the audience downward and away from the speaker's face. Learning to control your legs will avoid this distraction.

It's actually pretty easy, once you learn the speaker's stance. In the speaker's stance, your legs are shoulder width apart with your feet firmly planted and your toes pointing slightly outward. Your legs should be bent just a little bit (to avoid odd-looking locked legs), and your weight should be evenly distributed over both legs, not leaning toward one hip. Arms should be relaxed and at your sides. Avoid placing your hands behind your back, clasping them below your waist, or putting them in your pockets. This is a solid stance that communicates credibility and is not distracting.

If you have trouble keeping your legs planted firmly when you speak, practice by standing with your toes on two sheets of paper. Check back occasionally to see if you have moved off the paper. Also, *choose your shoes carefully*. Uncomfortable shoes, high heels, noisy shoes, and shoes that are too small can all make the problem of uncontrolled legs even worse.

STEP 8: MAKE EYE CONTACT

Eye contact is a challenge for some speakers, particularly among those who have come to the United States from cultures in which direct eye contact is rarely made. In the United States, we are expected to make eye contact with people when we are communicating with them. Here, looking someone in the eye shows respect and builds trust. If you avoid people's eyes, you may be perceived as uninvolved, rude, or even untruthful.

Ultimately, your goal is to sustain your eye contact with individual audience members for a complete thought before moving on to the next point. For now, work to look into the eyes of audience members while you are speaking. Be sure to look to both the left and right sides of the room, and not just at your instructor.

STEP 9: CONTROL YOUR VOICE

Your voice is the primary way you communicate your message. Controlling your rate and volume are essential parts of getting your message to your audience.

Many new speakers find themselves talking too quickly to be understood. This is a problem that also makes it hard to keep up your verbal fluency. Try to take your time as you speak. Remember to pause and breathe. Of course, you don't want to speak too slowly, but speeches delivered at a moderate pace are more likely to be understood and believed.

Additionally, make sure everyone in your audience can hear you. Be sure to spend time talking to the people in the back of the room. The volume you need to talk to them will be adequate for everyone else. Be sure to speak louder if you are in a large room or there is noise in the room such as an air conditioner.

More advanced vocal techniques will be covered in Chapter 13, but for now focus on controlling these basic aspects of your voice.

STEP 10: AVOID REPETITIVE NON-WORDS

Non-words are sounds like "um" and "uh" that find their way into our vocabulary during a speech. These filler sounds crop up because we are afraid of using silence in our delivery, so we make pointless sounds to keep the audience listening. The irony is that these sounds actually distract an audience from listening. The use of effective pausing during sentences is one of the best ways to keep an audience involved in your speech.

Non-words can also be words that we think are real words, but they are used during a speech like a filler word. Common examples of these are:

Like	**Y'know**	**Stuff**
So	**Okay**	**Basically**
Well	**And**	**Really**

These words weaken our content because they are meaningless when used as fillers or in excess.

You may not be aware that you are using non-words in your performances. Ask a classmate or review your speech on video to check. If you use a lot of them, deciding to make an effort to avoid these words is the first step to getting them out of your speeches. Also, be careful when you look at your note cards. This is a very common time when speakers will say, "Ummmmmm." When you feel the urge to use a non-word during a speech, just pause. Chances are it's a natural, necessary break in the idea you are discussing. Your delivery will go from cluttered to compelling!

The Top 10 Steps To Preparing & Delivering Your First Public Speech:

1. Care
2. Organize Your Thoughts
3. Start Strong/End Strong
4. Look Great/Feel Great
5. Show Your Personality
6. Never Drop the Ball
7. Control Your Body
8. Make Eye Contact
9. Control Your Voice
10. Avoid Repetitive Non-Words

Conclusion

This chapter has covered some of the basic elements for preparing and delivering your first speech. Some are more difficult than others, but everyone has the ability to do these in their speeches. Work to master these steps with each speech you give. Later in the term, you will begin applying more advanced techniques to your speaking style.

The best way to master these techniques is through practice. In the January 1994 *Communication Education,* Kent Menzel and Lori Carrell showed that speakers who spent time practicing for other people scored higher on their speeches and were rated as more skilled than those that didn't practice.

One word of caution: You can practice *too much* for a speaking event. This may make your speech sound wooden or insincere when you deliver it, because there is no spontaneity left in your delivery. It can also impact your mental state about giving the speech. Thinking too much about the speech, especially losing sleep because of it, can harm your brain's ability to stay focused and respond naturally.

When you are confident that you know your speech content, are within the assigned time limit, and have delivered a few solid run-throughs of your speech for practice audiences (such as your family), put your mind at ease and relax. Review your materials on the day of the speech and once or twice in the hour before your class meets. If you have prepared enough *beforehand*, speech day can actually be a very enjoyable and fun day.

Use these ten steps as a progress check for yourself throughout the semester. If you keep working on them, they can be a good way to track your progress from fright to might.

From FRIGHT to MIGHT Moment

Every one of the ten steps is designed to reduce your fear of public speaking. Following them will help you connect with your audience. Once you are connected, being the "center of attention" is easy because they support you! Preparation will also help reduce the unpredictability that can lead to fear.

Speakers' Secret

Some popular ways to practice learning the content of your speech include:

- Speaking into a tape recorder and listening to the tape several times
- Writing your speech or outline several times by hand
- Drawing a diagram of your speech so you have a visual picture of its content

Chapter 3: Terms & Concepts

Appearance Distraction
Approaching the front of the room
Caring about the topic
Credibility
Dressing for the presentation
"Dropping the ball"
Eye contact
Non-words
Practicing the speech
Preparation
Speaker's stance
Vocal control

Works Cited

Benassi, Marco. Six Steps to Speaking Success.

Dragseth, Debora. "The Seven Habits of Highly Ineffective Speakers." *Bismarck Tribune* 18 July 2000: 1C.

Menzel, Kent & Carrell, Lori. "The Relationship Between Preparation and Performance in Public Speaking." *Communication Education* 43 (1994): 17-27.

ACTIVITY #1: Understanding Chapter 3

Answer the following items as true or false.
Answers appear in Appendix C.

1.	Preparation impacts your speech content and delivery	T	F
2.	By doing a good job with your speech, the audience will care about your topic as much as you do.	T	F
3.	Every classroom speech should have a beginning, middle, and end.	T	F
4.	Studies show that your appearance is not important to the audience.	T	F
5.	Dropping the ball happens when you make a mistake while speaking, but is not the mistake itself.	T	F

Activity #2: Videotaped Self-Analysis

Videotape one of your class performances, either at home or during class. Review the tape three times:

The first time: Watch the tape with no sound. Observe your appearance and body control.

The second time: Turn your head away and just listen to your voice. How is your rate? Do you sound like you care? Is there personality in your voice?

The third time: Watch and listen at the same time. Make observations about your overall effectiveness.

Write a short paper analyzing your performance based on the Ten Simple Steps outlined in this chapter. Which did you do well? Which still need attention? Give specific examples, and don't be too hard on yourself. Hardly anyone likes to see him/herself on tape!

Activity #3: Preparation Checklist

Complete the following checklist to excel at your next speech:

- ☐ Carefully thought-out content and organization of the speech
- ☐ Prepared a speaking outline or manuscript
- ☐ Did at least one revision of outline or manuscript
- ☐ Prepared speaking notes or note cards
- ☐ Performed the speech for a live person or people at least once
- ☐ Timed the speech at least three times within the time limits for the assignment
- ☐ Memorized the first and last line of the speech
- ☐ Included personal touches or a sense of my personality in the speech
- ☐ Imagined the speech performance from start to finish with no mistakes
- ☐ Care about my topic, my audience and/or my grade and will clearly show it during speech
- ☐ The work I have done on this speech reflects the overall grade I hope to earn in this class

Congratulations! You are ready to give a great speech! Now relax and enjoy your class until it's your turn to speak.

Listening

Talk to the hand 'cause the face don't wanna hear it. - Dr. Evil, *Austin Powers: The Spy Who Shagged Me*

In what way is listening a particularly important skill for students?

An entire chapter devoted to the topic of listening may, at first, seem out of place in a textbook about public speaking. However, if you remember the communication model detailed in Chapter 1, the role of a receiver or listener is a necessary part of any communication scenario. In fact, without listeners, a speech really isn't a speech at all. Also, think about all the time outside of this class you spend listening to music, listening to family and friends, and paying attention to instructors. These are just a few examples of moments we find ourselves as the receivers of information. Research reported in a 1981 *Journal of Applied Communication Research* article confirms that you are likely to spend more than half of your waking hours listening. Before we speak, read, or write, we listen. Even as early as our days in the womb, we listen to our mother's heartbeat.

You might think that with all this time spent listening, we would be effective listeners. Unfortunately, many people are poor listeners. The authors of the 1983 book *Effective Listening* report that 48 hours after hearing a ten-minute speech, an average listener hears, comprehends, and retains only 25% of what they heard.

What's the Harm?

Non-listening or poor listening has several detrimental results. One of these is the **negative impact on the speaker**.

When a speaker looks into an audience and sees faces that are clearly distracted and uninvolved, he or she can be very disheartened. This unresponsiveness may even increase the speaker's anxiety. Often, audience members forget that they can be seen by the speaker and imagine themselves to be invisible "observers" of communication.

However, watching a public speaker is not like watching a television; your involvement (or lack thereof) matters.

Poor listening also has a **negative impact on the success of the communication event as a whole**. Without good listeners, the entire communication process breaks down. You have probably heard about Martin Luther King, Jr.'s "I Have a Dream" speech delivered at the Lincoln Memorial in Washington, D.C. at the height of the civil rights movement. Despite his outstanding speech content and delivery, the event might have been a total failure had the audience not listened attentively, understood his message, and responded passionately.

Finally, poor listening has a **negative impact on the listener.** Poor listeners are often perceived as being rude, self-involved, or even less intelligent.

It's easy to understand why. If we lose 75% of the content shared with us, we end up with some pretty distorted information. **Message distortions** occur when the messages that are received are fundamentally different than those that were sent. There are three common types of message distortion.

Message Distortions:

- Omission
- Addition
- Substitution

Omission means that the listener did not comprehend the entire message and is missing key elements. **Addition** occurs when the listener adds information and details from his or her own imagination. Finally, **substitution** occurs when the listener confuses the portion of the message they have heard with a different set of information and ideas.

We can easily embarrass ourselves on exams, at work, or in social situations when we fail to listen effectively and distort the messages we hear.

Clearly, listening is a vital element in the communication process, but also one which often needs improvement. To begin this improvement, we must first understand the process of listening itself.

The Five Stages of Listening

Listening is not as simple as it may seem. Once a speaker sends a message to a receiver, a five-stage process begins.

STAGE ONE: HEARING

Hearing is the first stage in the listening process. Hearing is the natural involuntary, physiological, passive process by which we take in sounds from the outside world and filter them through the inner workings of the ear.

Our listening skills can break down in the hearing stage. **Physical impairments** such as vision or hearing loss may impact the hearing stage of listening. Another negative factor can be **external noise**. External noise can include auditory and visual interference from outside the communication transaction. We've all heard the sound of a siren cut through a conversation. Because of this interruption, we didn't hear what was actually being said.

Five stages in the listening process:

- Hearing
- Selection
- Interpretation
- Evaluation
- Responding

STAGE TWO: SELECTION

In **selection,** we consider all the sounds we hear and then choose certain messages on which to focus and others to disregard.

During the selection process several factors impede effective listening. **Preoccupation** with concerns about family, employment, or even an upcoming social event can prevent a listener from selecting to focus on the message of the speaker. Researchers contend that at least once per minute we stop focusing on the immediate message and take a mental vacation.

Another challenge during the selection stage is **rapid thought**. According to the 1985 book *Listening* by Andrew D. Wolvin and Carolyn Gwen Coakley, while the average individual speaks at approximately 100-150 words per minute, the mind of the average listener can process up to 500 words per minute. This gives the listener a false impression that he or she can focus on other thoughts or messages and still follow the speaker. However, as you know if you've ever tried to carry on a conversation while watching a television show at the same time, this is extremely challenging and hard to maintain for more than a few minutes.

Message overload can also impact selection. When the brain has reached its limit of information, like too many complicated statistics or technical terms, the listener may stop paying attention to the message and focus on something else.

Finally, the **avoidance of difficult things** can be another obstacle to the selection process. If the speaker is discussing a topic that is too emotional to handle, or if the discussion appears to be too intellectual or complex, you may possibly think about other things or go on a "brain vacation."

STAGE THREE: INTERPRETATION

During **interpretation,** listeners assign meaning and begin to understand the speaker's message. We assign meanings through the filter of our particular life experiences, which are never exactly the same as others' life experiences.

An obvious example of a problem during this stage is **listening to a speech in an unfamiliar language**. While we may hear and select the speaker's message, our life experiences have not given us the language tools to interpret and understand the content. However, problems with interpretation extend beyond language barriers.

Sometimes listeners use their life experiences to make inferences about what a particular type of person will likely say, or how a particular type of speech will always sound. These listeners **jump to conclusions** – interpreting only a portion of the message and making faulty assumptions about the speaker or the content of the speech.

Even when we have the best intentions and try to interpret every detail, fact, and statistic presented, we **listen too intensively** and can miss the major concepts.

STEP FOUR: EVALUATION

In **evaluation**, the listener goes beyond simply interpreting messages and begins to draw conclusions based on certain questions: Is this information important? Is it appropriate? Is it true?

Evaluating the overall merit of a speech and a speaker is important. However, if you spend all your time focusing on the speaker's appearance and delivery or if you mentally argue and disagree with everything he or she says, then you are guilty of **overly critical listening.** If you are overly critical, you may start to rehearse arguments in your mind and stop paying attention to the speaker's words and ideas.

At the other extreme, **gullible listening** is accepting information at face value and not applying any critical thinking to what has been said. This can create disastrous results. A student in one of our classes gave a speech encouraging the class to obtain credit to establish a consumer credit history. Another student, without evaluating the message, signed up for several credit cards. By the end of the semester he was overextended and could not make his payments.

Also keep in mind that most audience members are self-centered. If it's not apparent or if a speaker does not explain why the information presented is important to listeners, the **lack of apparent advantages for listening** can cause audience members to evaluate messages negatively and stop listening altogether.

STAGE FIVE: RESPONDING

The final stage of listening is **responding**. Ideally in this stage, listeners respond to speakers with verbal and nonverbal cues that demonstrate their comprehension of the message presented. Remember that communication is a constant transaction between the sender and receiver, so we are responding at all times while we are listening.

Unfortunately, our responsiveness can break down in two key ways. First, listeners can give the speaker **negative feedback**. Frowning, snickering, or talking to a classmate while someone is speaking, sends the message that the speech (or the speaker) is not important. This lack of respect may cause the speaker to perform poorly on their assignment.

Second, even though most research suggests that we are poor listeners, we seem to be quite talented at **fake listening. Fake listening** occurs in part because we are expected to pay attention and be courteous audience members. We all know the fake listening cues. The head nod, the smile, and the courtesy laugh may give the impression that we are listening. However, if our minds are elsewhere, then we miss out on a chance to receive potentially valuable information.

General Listening Problems

There are two final ways in which listening breaks down and these can have an impact in any of the five stages of listening. First, **physiological problems,** including hunger, tiredness, or an upset stomach, can prevent the receiver from listening at maximum capacity. Second, our **lack of training** contributes immensely to our poor listening habits. According to an article in the *Washington Post* of February 20, 2001, less than 2% of adults have had any formal training in listening skills. Yet, listening requires instruction and practice in order to be successfully developed.

4 Kinds of Listening
- Appreciative {music}
- Empathic {emotion support}
- Comprehensive {lecture}
- Critical {jury in trial}

Improving Listening Skills

Decades of watching television and, more recently, interfacing with computers, have made Americans into more passive participants in communication settings. If you talk to your television, it won't talk back. **Passive listening** is listening without being engaged. This type of listening has few benefits because we do not force ourselves to grow and learn.

Active listening is listening that is engaged. This interactive participation is vital in effective communication. Don't hide behind someone or sit in the back. Consider some self-improvement of your listening skills in two areas: psychological and physical.

ACTIVE LISTENING IN THE MIND

Psychologically, you can optimize your ability to hear, select, interpret, evaluate, and respond to a message through a few simple steps. First, when a message is presented to you, simply **decide that it is time to listen.** Deciding to listen to the message eliminates some of the distractions in the selection stage. Every time you find yourself going "on a vacation," force yourself to return to the moment at hand.

Improving Listening Skills:

- Decide that it's time to listen
- Focus your listening
- Avoid jumping to conclusions
- Look for common ground with the speaker
- Place yourself in a listening position
- Use positive, responsive facial expressions
- Follow basic rules of courtesy

While the speech is underway, you can also **focus your listening**. Compare and contrast ideas and issues and engage in a mental review of the speaker's main points. Use the "extra" mental energy you have because of rapid thought to stay involved in the speech and avoid daydreaming. Also, paying careful attention to a speaker's evidence allows you to listen critically without sacrificing comprehension or being too gullible.

Finally, **avoid jumping to conclusions.** Delaying or avoiding judgment will allow you to fully hear the speaker's content. You can also **look for common ground with the speaker**. Identifying common interests you have with the speaker and/or the message will help account for the weight of your personal bias in the evaluation stage.

ACTIVE LISTENING IN THE BODY

When we are listening we are also communicating nonverbally, so it is essential to monitor our physical responsiveness. A simple technique is to **place yourself in a listening position**, which includes facing the speaker, making eye contact, and keeping your body position open by avoiding crossed arms or a hunched back. Additionally, **use positive, responsive facial expressions** to encourage the speaker and send the message that you are open to new ideas.

People who send positive and encouraging nonverbal messages to speakers are considered **supportive listeners.** As you give your speeches in this class, you will undoubtedly be grateful when you see friendly, interested, and smiling faces looking back at you from the audience.

Of course, we must also **follow basic rules of courtesy**, as well. Turn off cell phones and pagers, refrain from side conversations, and avoid distracting noises that impede hearing and selection.

Conclusion

In this chapter we have discussed the vitally important, yet often neglected, skill of listening. In the end, remember that just as it is important to care about speaking, you must also care about listening. *The Journal of Instructional Psychology*, December 1999, states that, "Good listeners stand out in the crowd; they are cherished by employers, teachers, friends, and others. They get promotions and are better informed than are poor listeners. The benefits of listening improvement are tangible and vital to success and self worth."

From FRIGHT to MIGHT Moment

Listening to your classmates' speeches is one of the best ways to reduce your nervousness on a big speech day. If you allow yourself to become involved in their messages, you won't be as likely to obsess about your own speech that is coming up.

Speakers' Secret

To avoid listening distractions, be sure to get enough rest.

Get adequate and regular sleep. A tired mind is an unfocused mind. Listening is KEY to learning, yet too many students are too tired to listen effectively.

Chapter 4: Terms & Concepts

Active Listening
Addition
External Noise
Fake Listening
Gullible Listening
Hearing
Jumping to Conclusions
Listening
Message Overload
Omission
Passive Listening
Preoccupation
Rapid Thought
Substitution
Supportive Listening

Works Cited

Holley, F. "An Investigation of Proportional Time Spent in Various Communication Activities by College Students." *Journal of Applied Communication Research* 8 (1981): 101-109.

Oldenburg, Don. "Now Hear This and Pay Attention." *Washington Post* 20 Feb. 2001: C4.

Petress, Kenneth. "Listening: A Vital Skill." *Journal of Instructional Psychology* 26 (1999): 261+.

Steil, Lyman K., Barker, Larry and Watson, Kittie. *Effective Listening.* Reading, MA: Addison-Wesley, 1983.

ACTIVITY #1: Understanding Chapter 4

Answer the following items as true or false.
Answers appear in Appendix C.

1. Most people interpret messages through a similar filter.	**T**	**F**
2. Humans can mentally process words faster than they can speak them.	**T**	**F**
3. There are four stages of listening.	**T**	**F**
4. Preoccupation can prevent a listener from focusing on the message of the speaker.	**T**	**F**
5. Sleep can prevent the receiver from listening at full capacity.	**T**	**F**

Activity #2: Class Observation

Ask an instructor on campus if you can sit in on 20-30 minutes of one of his/her classes during a lecture session. Sit near the back of the class and discreetly observe the listening behaviors of the students in class. Afterwards, answer each of the following questions:

1. What percentage of the students did you feel were listening actively and supportively?

2. What negative listening behaviors did you observe?

3. What positive listening behaviors did you observe?

4. What could be some of the likely outcomes of the listening behaviors of this class?

5. Why didn't the assignment ask you to observe students in a class in which you are enrolled?

Activity #3: Choosing Stimuli

Turn on your radio and television at the same time. Then, while both are still on, make a phone call to a friend and carry on a conversation. After five minutes, stop and write down as many messages as you remember hearing. Answer the following questions:

1. Which stimuli did you choose as your primary message?

2. Did you focus on one message or did you jump from one to another?

Topic Selection and Clarification

That's a very polished little speech... for a barbarian. -Barbara, *Red Dust*

What is a topic you feel you could talk about right now with no research or preparation?

Is that a good topic for a speech, or just an easy one?

If you were assigned to give an eight-minute informative speech to your class tomorrow, what would you choose to talk about? Chances are, you would select a topic with which you are already knowledgeable, but would that necessarily be the best topic? Perhaps you are given several weeks to write a speech. There are literally millions of potential topics to choose from. Could you spend too much time choosing your topic?

Topic Selection

In an effort to help you decide on the right topic for each speaking occasion in a reasonable amount of time, we've identified a simple three-step process to help you choose a topic.

STEP ONE: COMPILE A LIST OF POTENTIAL TOPICS

With the goal of the speech in mind, generate a list of as many potential topics as possible. First, **brainstorm** a list of topic ideas. Consider your hobbies, your educational experiences, magazine articles or books you have read, classes you have taken, and even places you have traveled. You may not find enough possible topics through brainstorming alone, though, so consider **researching** to find topic ideas. Browse magazine indexes, book racks, and web sites in general areas of interest to you. Then, collect more possible topics for your list. Finally, you may discover some great potential topics by simply **asking around.** Ask friends or family members for ideas. Your instructor for this class or in your other classes may have ideas to share with you, too.

STEP TWO: EVALUATE EACH TOPIC

Step two is perhaps the most important of these three steps. In order to ensure that your topic will be effective, evaluate your topic by asking these six questions:

Is it appropriate for the speaking situation or assignment? If you are asked to speak at a family reunion, you probably shouldn't deliver a serious persuasive speech about a controversial topic. The topic should be more entertaining and personal. Similarly, if your instructor asks you to prepare an informative demonstration speech, you wouldn't want to select a persuasive topic. Be sure that the topic you choose is right for the general goal of your speech.

Can I find enough research on this topic? To prepare a speech you will need a good understanding of your subject area. Your instructor will even assign you a minimum number of sources for some of your speeches in this class. Before you commit to a topic, be sure to do some investigation to see if you can find enough information about your topic to prepare a complete and supported speech.

Three Steps in Choosing a Topic:

1. Create a list of potential topics
2. Evaluate each topic on the list
3. Commit to one topic

Is it interesting to me? Am I motivated to work on this topic? Of course, it is important that you are interested in your topic. However, don't limit yourself to only speaking about issues that you already care deeply about (or know a lot about). The best speakers will search for topics, read about them, and develop an interest in some subjects that are new to them. There are probably some issues that you care about today that you didn't think much about a few years ago. How did you feel about school violence or airport security? Keep an open mind, and find ways to connect with topics that are completely new to you.

Will a speech on this topic be exciting or interesting for my audience? Have you ever had to sit through hours and hours of someone else's vacation slideshow? If so, you probably understand the importance of choosing a topic that has some interesting and exciting elements for your audience. It's not always obvious if a topic is interesting, though. Think about how you would present the speech. Could you use interesting visual aids? Are there compelling stories that would keep the audience involved? A few years ago, a student from Bradley University, Edwin Reed, won a National Informative Speaking Championship with a speech about *whey* – the milky byproduct created when cheese is made.

He used humor and fascinating stories and examples and kept the audience glued to their seats for the whole performance.

Does the topic have a direct or indirect impact on my audience? A good topic will go beyond just being interesting and will also be important (or *significant*) to the audience in some way. For instance, you could consider whether the topic will help your audience live a safer, happier, or healthier life. Will it help them make more money, have better financial security, or get a better job? Will it give them insights into a new culture or increase their understanding and acceptance of others? Will it challenge them to think about a timely issue, or teach them about an important new development that will influence their lives in the future? Will it provide them with an opportunity for emotional release? Be sure your topic will have a significant payoff for your audience by the end of the speech. You don't want to speak and then be immediately forgotten.

Is the topic area too large to cover in my allotted time? Finally, a common mistake that speakers make is to select topics that are too broad. Could you really talk comprehensively about "television" in an eight-minute speech? You could speak for hours and not thoroughly inform your audience about "television." It's better to choose a topic that you can reasonably cover in your allotted time. Narrow your focus to a subset of the original area. For instance, more suitable topics in the area of "television" might include "violence in children's cartoon shows," or "how a television works," or "advances in high definition television." You will probably find it much easier to write a speech with a narrow topic area.

Evaluating a Topic:

- Is it appropriate for the situation/assignment?
- Is it researchable?
- Is it interesting to me?
- Will it be interesting to my audience?
- Is it important/relevant for my audience?
- Can it be covered within my time limit?

If you answer "no" to any of the questions above, get rid of the topic and try another until you find one that meets all six criteria.

STEP THREE: COMMIT TO ONE TOPIC

Although it might be scary, commit to a topic as early as possible. Your instructor may want to approve your topic for each assignment, as well. Try to complete this step as early in the speechmaking process as possible to give yourself plenty of time to develop the content of the speech. It is also important not to switch topics late in the process. Sometimes speakers find a new topic idea just a few days before a major assignment and change their topic – often with disastrous results.

Once you have made your choice of topic, it is time to clarify exactly what you will be speaking about by writing out your **general goal**, **specific purpose,** and **topic revelation** statements.

Topic Clarification

Remember from Chapter One that most speeches have one of three general goals. These are almost always expressed as one of the following statements:

General Goal:	***To inform***
General Goal:	***To persuade***
General Goal:	***To entertain***

The **specific purpose** of your speech is a longer statement that explains in much greater detail what you will accomplish during your speech. You may use the following formula to write your specific purpose:

> Your general goal + the audience to whom you are speaking + a precise description of your topic area = Specific Purpose

For example:

Specific Purpose: ***To persuade my classmates to complete their drivers' license organ donor cards***

Finally, the **topic revelation statement** of your speech is a summary sentence explaining the specific content area you will discuss during your speech. The important thing to remember about a topic revelation statement so you won't confuse it with the general goal or the specific purpose is that the topic revelation statement is *phrased to be spoken to your audience.* It is also *written in a complete sentence.* The topic revelation statement will actually appear in the text of your speech introduction.

The topic revelation statement is possibly the most important sentence in your whole speech. If the audience doesn't recognize it when they hear it, they may struggle to understand the point of your speech. Starting with a **time indicator** is a good way to draw the audience to your topic revelation statement. This is a word or short phrase that creates a sense of immediacy about the topic revelation statement. Some examples are, "Today," "In the next few minutes," or "This afternoon."

Next, make your topic revelation statement active by adding a phrase with a good **communicating verb** – a verb that actively expresses your function as a speaker. The easiest choice might seem to be the verb from your general goal statement. For instance, "I will inform you about…" Of course, you should not ever say to an audience, "I will persuade you." It could create some defensiveness, so try a more accessible option: "I will argue that…" or "I will make the case that..." or even "I hope to persuade you that…" Some other good communicating verbs include:

Describe	**Present**
Demonstrate	**Offer**
Reveal	**Assert**
Tell	**Shock**
Express	**Challenge**
Show	**Defend**

Finally, consider adding a few adjectives to make your topic more vivid. Next, combine your time indicator and communicating verb with the specific purpose of your speech. You should now have a clear, concise, and direct topic revelation statement that really gets the attention of the audience.

Topic Revelation Statement: ***Today I hope to convince you to complete your organ donor card, a generous, life-saving action for people of all ages.***

In order to help you understand the process of choosing a topic, as well as writing your general goal, specific purpose, and topic revelation statement, let's consider the example of an actual student named Herman.

Herman was assigned an informative speech. He created a long list of topics (step one) by brainstorming and speaking with one of his biology teachers. One of the topics on the list was "bugs."

Next, he evaluated the topics (step two). Although he decided that bugs are a topic of potential interest to his audience, and he liked them personally, he found that the topic was not suitable for his time limit of 8 minutes. It was just too broad. Imagine how long it would take to actually cover the topic of "bugs" thoroughly! It's not possible to *name* every bug on earth in 8 minutes, or even 8 hours.

Herman narrowed his focus to cockroaches. And because he was speaking to a general audience, he decided to steer clear of complicated anatomical and biological aspects of the cockroach and instead focus his presentation on how scientists are using cockroaches to solve crimes, a branch of science known as forensic entomology.

Now he was ready to commit to his topic (step three) and clarify his topic. First, he wrote his general goal.

General Goal: ***To inform***

Next, he wrote his specific purpose.

Specific Purpose: ***To teach my classmates about the role cockroaches can play in helping forensic scientists solve crimes.***

Now Herman had to explain the topic area of his speech in language suitable for his audience – his topic revelation statement:

Topic Revelation Statement: ***Today, I will introduce you to an unusual new detective on the crime scene investigation team– the cockroach.***

After you have selected a topic and composed your general goal, specific purpose, and topic revelation statement, you are ready to start your own detective work. Carefully analyze your audience and research your topic area (Chapters 6 and 7) so you will be able to compose the best possible speech.

From FRIGHT to MIGHT Moment

Choosing a good topic can help overcome speech anxiety. A topic that is interesting and relevant to the audience will help ensure that they are focused on your message instead of you.

Speakers' Secret

When choosing a topic for a class speech, keep an open mind.

It has been said that, *"The mind is like a parachute. It only operates when open."* Take the opportunity to learn about many topics. Become involved in many new subject areas. Allow yourself to *become* enthused about a new topic.

Chapter 5: Terms & Concepts

Brainstorming
Communicating Verb
Specific Purpose
Time Indicator
Topic Analysis
Topic Revelation Statement

ACTIVITY #1: Understanding Chapter 5

Answer the following items as true or false.
Answers appear in Appendix C.

1.	There are three steps in choosing a topic.	T	F
2.	When evaluating a topic, it is never appropriate to examine whether or not a topic is researchable.	T	F
3.	The three general goals of speech making are to entertain, inform, and excite.	T	F
4.	Make your topic revelation statement active by adding a phrase with a good communicating adjective.	T	F
5.	A few action verbs help make people understand the importance of your topic.	T	F

ACTIVITY #2: Topic Evaluation

Imagine that you have been asked to give a 6-8 minute informative demonstration speech for a third grade class in your community. You have come up with some possible topics, but aren't sure which is best. Complete the following chart to find the best topic(s) for this speaking occasion:

TOPIC IDEA:	Is it APPROPRIATE FOR THE SITUATION/ ASSIGNMENT?	Is it RESEARCHABLE?	Is it INTERESTING TO YOU?	Will it be INTERESTING TO MY AUDIENCE?	Is it IMPORTANT AND RELEVANT to my audience?	Can it be covered within my TIME LIMIT?	If it meets all the criteria, you have a GREAT TOPIC!
The history of the United States							
Don't drink soda.							
How to play dodge ball							
Preparing your own tax returns							
My vacation to China							

Audience Analysis

You know, at the beauty academy they teach us that people aren't black or white or yellow or red, but their hair can be. - LuAnne, *King of the Hill*

The most successful speakers are able to relate to their listeners because they have developed an audience profile that delineates characteristics such as gender, age, ethnicity, religion, and socioeconomic status. The way to establish this profile is through audience analysis. The more you know about the individuals listening to your speech, the greater your chances of successfully communicating to them. This information allows you to adapt the message to a specific group of listeners and predicts the maximum impact your message will carry.

When you watch a speaker, what do you expect her to understand about you and your needs?

How do you feel when a speaker only tells you information you already know?

It is essential for the speaker to realize that audience members are self-centered to the extreme. Audience members might be pictured as rising up en masse and saying, "What's in it for me?" To answer this question, the effective speaker will be prepared to provide the audience the justification needed.

Types of Audience Analysis

DEMOGRAPHIC ANALYSIS

The first consideration is the *demographic profile* of the audience. Demographic analysis includes the statistical make up of the audience.

One of the first demographic issues to consider is the **gender** of the audience. Your topic selection may be altered if you anticipate speaking to mostly men, women, or a mixed audience. In addition to traditional identifications, gender has grown to include cross-cultural gender divisions of gay, lesbian, and transgender. You should never assume that someone holds any particular belief or engages in any specific behavior based on his or her gendered appearance. Simply being aware that differences in gender exist, however, will help you refrain from offending or isolating audience members.

Cultural factors are important to consider in all aspects of speechmaking, particularly in regards to delivery. Different cultural beliefs about verbal and nonverbal behavior can change the outcome of the message. For instance, in many Asian cultures direct eye contact with a new acquaintance is considered disrespectful. Yet, in the American public speaking arena, speakers are expected to establish direct eye contact with listeners. Also, if you know that an audience speaks a language different from your own, you may want to learn a few key words or phrases to help you communicate respect. President George W. Bush's use of the Spanish language during the 2002 presidential campaign may have actually helped him win critical votes from our Spanish-speaking population.

Age is an important factor in understanding how a message might be interpreted. Each generation has its own cultural experiences that seem to identify it as a unique group. For example, members of older generations can tell you where they were when John F. Kennedy was assassinated. Most students identify differently with this example because they were not born when JFK was alive and have only knowledge from writings and movies about him. Speakers should be particularly aware of audience age variables in selecting examples to share during presentations.

Demographic Issues:

- Gender
- Cultural factors
- Age
- Religious affiliation
- Educational level
- Work experience
- Socioeconomic status
- Political affiliation
- Relationship status
- Memberships

Religious affiliation, for many, is a deeply held value. Therefore, knowledge of the religious beliefs of the members of the audience is valuable in creating the speech. Certain topics could be perceived either positively or negatively simply because of a listener's religious commitment. Mandatory death sentencing is a topic that would have to be approached differently depending on the spiritual make-up of the audience.

The **educational level** of audience members is also important to consider. The complexity of your topic and your use of vocabulary, literary allusions, and historical facts should vary according to the educational level of your audience.

Work experience can be a helpful indicator of the different interests and knowledge an audience member would have concerning a topic. Workers have certain types of experiences because of their jobs. To overlook this vast source of knowledge would be to limit a valuable tool in developing effective speeches.

The **socioeconomic status** of audience members is also a valuable indicator of a certain range of content possibilities. An individual earning $100,000 per year will have different experiences and expectations than one earning less than $10,000 per year. Individuals with differing amounts of expendable income would receive a casual reference to visiting Paris differently.

Political affiliation is one of the standard ways to evaluate an audience. People join a political organization because it matches their beliefs and ideologies. The organization then reinforces those values that drew the person to become affiliated with that organization in the first place. The speaker would be wise to uncover these relationships.

The **relationship status** of individual audience members will assist you in addressing certain issues. As you prepare your speech you would want to know whether members of the audience are single, married, or living with someone.

Memberships in interest groups and community organizations will reveal certain information about audience members. Sierra Club members would approach the topic of waste management differently than members of a board of a construction company. Also, members of your audience will have a wide array of hobbies and interests, which will shed light on their interest in certain topics.

SITUATIONAL ANALYSIS

Determining the demographic makeup of an audience is important, but audience analysis should not stop there. You should also consider the specific speaking context. You must conduct **situational analysis**.

Factors in situational analysis include the **physical environment.** Make sure to consider things such as temperature, seating arrangement, seating comfort, lighting, and acoustics. If you are speaking to audience members in the middle of summer in Arizona and the air conditioning in the building stops working, the message may not be as effective as you would hope.

The **size** of the audience makes a difference in how the speech is delivered. Small, intimate speaking situations call for a different style than large, formal groups. Most experts agree that a conversational approach is used when communicating with just a few (1-5) people. For instance, it is probably more appropriate to sit alongside your audience instead of standing in these situations. Conversely, audiences larger than sixty usually necessitate amplification (depending on the type of space in which the speech occurs).

Finally, speakers must be concerned with the **attitude** of the audience toward the topic, speaker, occasion, and the event. Speaking for an eager and supportive audience is far different than speaking for a hostile and exhausted audience. The demeanor of students enrolled in a required traffic school will undoubtedly be different from the demeanor of students in a "How to Spend Your Lottery Winnings" course. Your speech must recognize and adapt to the different attitudes of your audiences.

This chapter presents just a few of the ways in which you can try to understand your audience better so you can reach them more effectively with your ideas. There are many more ways than you will find here in which you might want to analyze your audience. For instance, your **zip code** is actually considered to be one of the most telling bits of data about you. Advertisers depend on zip code lists to tell them everything from the type of car you probably drive, to how much fresh fruit you are likely to eat, right down to the brand of toothpaste you probably use.

If you plan to work in fields such as politics, television programming, business marketing, or advertising, you will undoubtedly learn much, much more about the ways in which an audience can be studied.

Gathering Information About the Audience

A speaker must collect audience **data** in order to prepare an effective speech. This can be done using surveys and interviews.

SURVEYS

Surveys can reveal valuable demographic and situational information. There are several types of survey questions. A **forced alternative** survey item makes it easy to tabulate results because there are usually just 2 or 3 possible answers to a question.

A **scale survey item** asks audience members to rate their opinions on a scale such as, "from one to ten." Be sure to indicate if ten is *good* or *bad.*

A Scale Survey Item:

Please circle the word(s) that indicate how you feel about the following statement:

Medical insurance should be provided to all United States citizens.

Strongly Agree Agree Neutral Disagree Strongly Disagree

There are other types of survey items, too, such as **open-ended questions** that ask respondents to write out words, phrases or even paragraphs to answer broad questions. These are very difficult types of items to tabulate into useful results because interpreting this type of data can be very subjective, and reading long responses can be very time-consuming.

INTERVIEWS

Interviews can also be a beneficial tool for audience analysis. Typically, you will have too many people in your audience to interview each person, so it is important to choose a small sample of audience members who will represent the audience for your speech.

Interviews can be scheduled in advance or can be done as late as a few minutes before the speech. A professional public speaker in the Los Angeles area makes a habit of conducting what she calls "shake and ask" interviews by wandering through her audience before the speech starts. She shakes hands with people and asks them questions like, "So – are you in the mood to laugh?" or "Who's the craziest person working in this company?" The responses help her shape the tone and content of her speech.

When you write questions for an audience analysis interview, be sure to keep the questions short and to the point. As you listen to responses to these questions, be sure to note both the verbal and the nonverbal responses given.

Using Audience Analysis Data

When using audience analysis data, one caution is to avoid **stereotyping**. A stereotype is an oversimplified picture of people different from us, particularly those from another race or culture. As information is gathered, individual variations within the group must be accounted for so that a unique and fair evaluation takes place. Audience analysis is a good guide but if you are too simplistic in your use of it, you may offend members of the audience that don't fit the generalization you've created.

After you collect information about the audience, you will want to consider shaping your speech in a number of different ways based on knowledge gained from audience analysis. The box to the left summarizes some of the key choices you must make. Let audience analysis guide these choices.

Some Uses of Audience Analysis in Preparing for a Speaking Event:

- Topic selection, focus and approach
- Language choices
- Structure and length of the speech
- Use of visuals and interaction
- Anticipating problems
- Appearance choices
- Examples used during the speech
- Avoiding awkward or embarrassing remarks
- Appealing to specific audience needs and desires

Conclusion

In this chapter, we have discussed the concept of analyzing your audience while preparing a speech. Types of audience analysis include demographic and situational. Information is gathered about the audience through surveys and interviews. Remember to exercise caution when using audience analysis to avoid overgeneralizations and stereotyping. As you continue to work through the chapters of this book, don't forget audience analysis. Every choice you make in preparing and delivering your speech should be filtered through the simple premise of, "Is this the best way to reach my audience?" After all, the phrase, "Speak for yourself" just isn't really the right approach. We speak for our *audience.*

From Fright to MIGHT Moment

Knowing your audience is the key to reducing speech anxiety. Conducting audience analysis ensures that you are focusing on them and not yourself. Audience analysis will also make your message more likely to reach your audience, which is the true measure of success for a public speaker.

Speakers' Secret

The more you know about your audience, the more successful you will be.

- Plan your surveys to be completed at least one week before your speech is due.
- When doing research for the speech topic, utilize audience analysis that has been conducted by professional organizations.

Chapter 6: Terms & Concepts

Age
Demographic Analysis
Educational Level
Gender
Income
Interviews
Memberships
Physical Environment
Political affiliation
Religious affiliation
Religious Affiliation
Surveys
Work Experience

ACTIVITY #1: Understanding Chapter 6

Answer the following items as true or false.
Answers appear in Appendix C.

1. Age, gender, ethnicity, religion, and socioeconomic status are important to understanding audience analysis.	T	F
2. Demographic analysis includes the statistical make up of the audience.	T	F
3. The educational level of the audience is not usually an important consideration.	T	F
4. Political affiliation is one of the standard ways to evaluate an audience.	T	F
5. Surveys can reveal valuable demographic and situational information.	T	F

ACTIVITY #2: The Difference Between Stereotyping and Audience Analysis

Complete the following table to help clarify some of the differences between stereotyping and sound audience analysis.

Observed or studied audience characteristic	A stereotype of this group that would be harmful to use in your speech preparation	A reasonable conclusion you might draw for shaping your speech
Mostly 60-year old people	They will all be hard-of-hearing so I will have to say my speech really loud!	I could use examples in my speech from the mid-1950's when they were teenagers.
All women		
Mostly Republicans		
All Caucasians (white)		
All Star Trek Fans		
College students		

ACTIVITY #3: Class Survey

Imagine that a guest speaker will be coming to your class in a few weeks and wants to prepare thoroughly for the occasion. He/she needs your help in understanding the audience and speaking context.

Your instructor will assign you a category of audience analysis from the list below. If the class is large, some students may need to work in pairs.

Number of students	**Employment status**	**Seating arrangement**
Gender	**Employment type**	**Stress level of students**
Ethnic background	**Socio-economic status**	**Taboo topics**
Religious affiliation	**Education level**	**Formality of attire**
Degree of religious involvement	**Relationship status**	**Temperature of room**
Nationality	**Age**	**Lighting & acoustics**
Political affiliation	**Memberships of students**	**Size of room**

Determine an appropriate method for collecting data about your classmates in your category of analysis. You may wish to use visual observation, a sampling of your classmates, or a census (asking everyone in the class). You will need to decide if you will ask yes/no, open-ended, or closed-ended questions. Some topics may be sensitive. How can you tactfully collect accurate data?

Collect your data and review your findings, then prepare a very short statement of your findings for a potential guest speaker in your classroom.

FOLLOW-UP QUESTION: If a guest speaker for your class wasn't able to get information like you have just provided from students in the class, what other options would he/she have for conducting audience analysis for this occasion?

Research and Support

Does our relationship warrant long - term commitment? I need some kind of proof, some kind of verifiable, empirical data. – John Nash, *A Beautiful Mind*

The central idea and main points for a speech are like a skeleton. A skeleton is a good start, but not much use (except on Halloween) without some muscles to keep it standing and make it move. In speech, the muscles are called **support.** Support in a speech can take on many forms. Sometimes it's a vivid description or a detailed personal story. Other times it could be hard facts or compelling testimony (in the form of a direct quotation) by a credible specialist. Your professor will discuss each type of support in class, and you can practice using each of the types in the activity later in this chapter.

What is a type of speech for which your own experience is probably the only kind of "research" you need to use?

Any time you prepare a speech, you will need to explore different areas to come up with support for your information and arguments. No major idea in your speech should be presented without support. Sometimes these major ideas are called **"claims."**

The easiest sources of support to use are examples from your own life experience and logical reasoning. **Personal experience** is the information we have accumulated through our observations and experiences including educational, professional, and family encounters. We often call this first-hand experience. Many students have relied on their personal experiences to create excellent speeches for class. Some sample topics include giving birth to a baby, coping with the death of a friend or family member, returning to Taiwan for a visit, turning twenty-one, attending the Academy Awards, celebrating Quinciñiera and describing Kwanzaa. While personal experience can be a valuable tool for creating your speech, most of the time, you will want to do some research to either increase your knowledge of the topic or understand an alternate perspective.

Often, though, you need more, *much more*, to support a speech than just what you already know about a topic, so you need to conduct **research.**

Sources of Research

The widespread use of computers has made research gathering incredibly easy. You have many different sources at your disposal, usually on your own campus, and maybe in the privacy of your home. There are three sources of research to consider.

LIBRARY AND DATABASE RESEARCH

Though the Internet has made it possible to access amazing amounts of information from our homes, it is important to remember that the libraries in our communities and on our campuses have great resources for speeches. They are also staffed with knowledgeable people who can help you if you hit a road block while gathering materials.

Since the library houses a large collection of books, one of its main resources will be the **catalog**. Nearly all libraries have computerized their catalogues, so a simple search can quickly produce a large number of results. Unless you know the title or author of the book you are looking for, you will probably search by **keyword,** which is a critical word or phrase that is contained in either the title of the book or its description. Simply type in the subject matter of your speech (or a related term) and examine the results. Add keywords if you get too many results, and subtract words if you get too few results.

Keep in mind that among the library's books will be reference guides such as almanacs, biographical indices, encyclopedias, periodical and newspaper abstracts or indices. These can be valuable sources of statistics or background information on your topic, so don't forget to check them out. Your instructor may have information on specific reference guides that he or she prefers students to use.

If your topic is fairly new or cutting-edge, you may have difficulty finding related books. Most libraries, however, have regularly updated computer databases that have full-text versions of magazine and newspaper articles, newswire releases, and television/radio transcripts. Databases such as ArticleFind, EBSCO, Infotrac, ProQuest, and Lexis-Nexis are updated weekly or daily and will contain the most recent information on many topics.

Searching these databases can be a bit tricky, as they can often produce too few or too many results to manage. To become an expert, consider attending a research class or orientation at your library. In the meantime, employ a few simple tips to make your searching more productive.

Learn some simple Boolean search terms such as "AND" "OR" and "NOT." You can use these words to connect two ideas and narrow down very broad topics (e.g., baseball AND rules).

Search within a date range. Most databases allow you to search within a set of dates (e.g., after 2000). Start with the most recent dates and work your way back if you don't find enough information.

Use quotation marks. If a phrase or group of words is placed in quotation marks, typically a database will only find those articles that have that exact phrase or words. This will reduce the number of articles found and increase the usefulness of the results.

Follow the directions for the database you are using. Often a few minutes spent learning how to optimize your search will save you hours of time sorting through irrelevant results.

WEB-BASED RESEARCH

The World Wide Web and Internet have become extremely popular sources of research. Let's face it, nearly anyone can have a web page, which makes the Internet both a blessing and a curse when doing your research.

The web is a fantastic resource simply because of the amount of information available. Complete versions of most major newspapers and magazines are available on the web. So is a great amount of information from local, state, and national governments. Colleges, universities, and corporations publish tremendous amounts of research and information on their websites as well. These are all excellent places to look for information about your topic.

For every legitimate piece of information on the web, there is at least one suspect or false bit of information. This is largely due to the fact that the open nature of the web makes it difficult to have any kind of editorial control. When a newspaper or magazine is published, its articles are carefully checked and edited for accuracy. Often websites, especially personal ones, lack the careful research and fact checking that makes published materials reliable. Therefore, the burden of checking accuracy and reliability falls on *you* when researching on the web.

There are several things to consider when evaluating websites.

Look for clues to good information. Does the website include the date the information was published or updated? Is the author clearly identified? Does the site give any information about the author's credentials or experience? Is the information on the site consistent with other sources you have found?

Identify the presenter of the information. What organization is sponsoring or presenting this material? What can you find out about that organization's goals?

Whenever you evaluate a website, consider the domain name and extension. These are contained in the site's address and usually provide clues about who is providing the information you have accessed.

Some common domain names are listed below.

.gov – Websites of local, state, or federal governments, usually containing official information.

.edu – Websites of colleges and universities. May contain official college pages, homepages of faculty/staff, and student homepages. Consider who at the college is publishing the information.

.org – Websites of organizations that range from charitable to professional to political. Consider the organization's goals when evaluating information.

.net – Originally intended for technical websites, this extension is now available to anyone and is often used by Internet Service Providers for personal web pages (e.g., earthlink.net).

.com – Often business or commercial websites, but may also be personal websites set up through internet services (e.g., aol.com).

While web research has become popular, it is not always the best source of information for your speech. Often students use the web exclusively because of its convenience. Don't forget there are libraries and databases available to you that may have more information and will probably be better organized in helping you access it. Find the best facts for your *audience*, not simply the most convenient information available! Your instructor may also have specific guidelines or limits for web based research, and you can also find additional resources in Appendix C of this book.

INTERVIEWS

In addition to published materials, you may want to consider interviewing an expert on your topic as a source of research. An expert may provide you with information not available in published material or give you insight into a facet of your topic you haven't considered. Always brainstorm potential people to interview for your speech topics. Aim high – inventors, authors, and even politicians are often willing to talk to students if they know they are doing research for a class.

If you choose to do an interview, it is important to remember that you are using someone else's time. Consider the best way to contact the person: a letter, phone or e-mail. Follow these guidelines if you are planning an interview.

Contact the person well in advance of your speech. You may have difficulty scheduling a time to interview them. Don't leave lengthy messages asking the person to call you. Try another time.

Prepare your questions ahead of time. Prior to contacting the person, know what you want to ask, in case they say "now" is the best time for an interview.

Be courteous and professional during the interview. Dress appropriately and treat the person you are interviewing with respect.

Ask permission if you plan to record the interview. It is illegal to tape record a conversation without permission.

Be sure to thank the person for the interview. You may also want to send a note after the interview is over.

Immediately after the interview organize your notes. Write out the parts you want to remember and include in your speech. If you wait to do so, you may forget what the person said.

Whatever method(s) of research you choose, keep in mind that research is only the first step to completing your speech. You still have to use the research you have gathered in your speech. To do so, it is important to identify some ways to support your ideas that may be contained in your research.

Supporting Materials

During your speech, you will present to your audience many ideas. These ideas were referred to earlier as "claims." Few of these claims will be accepted by the audience without any kind of explanation. For example, if you tell the audience that safety regulations for playground equipment are insufficient, you have made an important claim. But does your audience understand how or why this equipment is dangerous? Will your audience accept this statement just because you have said it?

By drawing on research materials, you can make your claims more powerful for your audience. Supporting materials can enhance your speech in three ways, known as the three C's.

Clarity. Complex or difficult ideas will be easier to understand with supporting materials. A simple explanation or analogy can turn a confusing point into one your whole audience comprehends.

Color. Audiences are bombarded with tons of information every day. Your supporting materials can help distinguish your claims from all the others. A powerful example, story, or statistic may stick in an audience's mind and help them to remember the speech long after it is over.

Credibility. People will rarely believe something just because you have said it. The backing of your research and supporting materials proves to the audience that, while you may not be an expert on your topic, you have taken the time to learn about it. It also shows you consulted those who are experts. Demonstrating this to your audience makes it easier for them to believe the claims you will make.

CONVERTING RESEARCH INTO SUPPORT

Now that you know some of the ways supporting materials can improve your speech, let's consider how to turn the research you've gathered into usable supporting materials.

The first step is to **read all of your research.** It is important that you view all facets of your topic before you decide to focus on just a few. You need to have a complete understanding of your topic before you can explain it to others.

After you have read all of your research, you should **identify supporting materials.** You can do this by highlighting or underlining key parts of the articles and books that you may include in your speech. Figuring out which parts are most important requires being familiar with the types of supporting material.

TYPES OF SUPPORTING MATERIAL

Definitions are one type of supporting material that can be particularly effective for difficult concepts. If your speech is about a scientific or technical subject, for example, you will probably need to define some terms that are unfamiliar to the audience. Keep in mind, though, that not all definitions have to be **denotative**, or the literal definition from the dictionary. You can define through description, example, or just by putting something in your own words.

Descriptions are supporting materials that appeal to our senses. They use creative and colorful language to make a concept come alive for an audience. When the audience can experience your spoken words through their senses of smell, touch, sight, sound and taste, they are more likely to be affected by your idea and remember it when you are finished. If your speech is about the Australian Outback, your audience will be far more affected if you give vivid details about the sights and sounds of this area instead of just offering facts.

Explanations differ from descriptions by appealing to our curiosity and capacity for reason. They often focus on clarifying the reason something occurs or how an item works. For example, a speech about a new technique for fighting cancer will resonate more with the audience if they know how the treatment actually works in the body.

Examples are very versatile and effective means of support because they show the audience an idea in real terms. They can be used to personalize or make human the point at hand. They also are used to clarify or reinforce a point. Notice that throughout this book, the authors have provided examples for most concepts to show you in real terms how they can be applied to a speech. Examples may be brief, a mention of a name or no more than a sentence. They may also be detailed, sometimes taking up a whole main point of your speech. Regardless, make sure your examples are relevant to your speech.

There are three different types of examples.

Factual examples have actually happened. They are examples of real people or real situations. The audience does not have to be familiar with the people or situations involved, but you should relate the example to the audience.

Hypothetical examples are created by the speaker. They can be used to get the audience to imagine themselves in a specific scenario. Hypothetical examples should contain lots of details and description to truly have the audience create a mental picture. If you want to maximize the effectiveness of your scenario, avoid using the words "Imagine yourself…" You break the illusion of reality when you tell the audience to imagine, and if your words are vivid enough, your audience will already be creating a mental picture!

Extended examples are longer examples that have more detail. An extended example may take up an entire point of a speech, using aspects of the story to make the smaller points. Another common use of an extended example is one that recurs throughout the speech. It may begin in the introduction, return to make a point in the body, and conclude the speech.

Statistics are numerical data. Even though people may dislike math and numbers, they still like to see concepts put in numerical terms. If you tell an audience that something costs a lot of money, their natural response will be, "how much?" If you tell them a lot of people believe something is true, they will wonder, "how many?" That's where statistics play an important role. They can clarify or expand an idea by adding quantitative backing. Some statistics you may use include ratios, averages, and percentages. Follow these guidelines for using statistics in your speech:

Make sure your statistics are from a reliable source. Any support should be from a good source, but your statistics are especially important to check. The way they are generated, compiled, and reported all contribute to your credibility.

Identify the source of your statistics. Not only will this add to your credibility, it is also your ethical responsibility. Someone or some group took the time to produce the statistics you are citing. Remember from Chapter One, you must give proper credit to the source or you are committing plagiarism.

Use numbers and units your audience can understand. If your audience is primarily American, units such as kilometers, grams, or francs will be meaningless to them. Take the time to convert your numbers to familiar units. Additionally, round off numbers. Your audience doesn't need to know that 48.779% of people believe something. Simply saying 48.8 or 49% will be easier for the audience to comprehend.

Explain and clarify your statistics. It is not enough to just present a number to the audience. Make sure your speech explains the meaning or impact of the statistic to the audience. You may want to consider relating the statistic to your audience. Put a percentage in human terms (e.g., "Three out of four students receives financial aid. That means that roughly 25 people in this class get some form of assistance.") or tell the audience how a statistic may affect them. Since statistics can often be confusing, make sure your numbers improve the audience's understanding of your topic.

Types of Supporting Materials:

- Definitions
- Descriptions
- Explanations
- Examples
- Statistics
- Testimony
- Comparison/Contrast
- Visual Aids

Testimony quotes or paraphrases an individual. These statements may be from an interview that you conducted, or taken from one of your printed sources. You may choose to use the words of average people, also known as **lay testimony.** You may choose the words of a specialist to prove a point. This is known as **expert testimony.** Any time you use testimony, inform your audience of the person's qualifications, which may include their experience or education. If your audience understands the person you are quoting is qualified to speak about that subject, they will be more likely to believe the testimony.

Comparison/Contrast is a form of support that relates an unfamiliar idea to one the audience knows. It may also be referred to as an **analogy.**

In a comparison, the speaker points out the similarities between the two concepts. When contrasting, the speaker highlights the differences. There are two common forms of comparison.

A **literal comparison** describes actual similarities between concepts that share physical or observable characteristics. This type of comparison is useful when comparing two programs or two policies. It is often used when comparing objects, events, or people. For example, a speaker might say, "The students in Japan are quite similar to American students except that they attend school more hours per day and six days per week."

A **figurative comparison** relates objects or ideas that may appear to have nothing in common. You may know it as a simile or metaphor. It compares the relationships between the unrelated items and asks the audience to make the connection more concrete. For example, a speaker might say, "The student of today is like a juggler trying to keep all her plates in the air at one time. Between work, school, family, friends, and church, she is always struggling to balance her many activities and responsibilities."

Visual Aids support an idea by appealing to another of the audience's senses. They already hear your ideas, but visual aids allow them to see your ideas, too. Visual aids may both clarify an idea and make it more vivid for your audience.

Citing Sources

A critical part of using support in a speech is to give credit in the speech to the source from which you obtained the information. This is called a *source citation* or "cite," for short. Using cites adds credibility to you and your ideas, and is your ethical responsibility as a speaker.

Citing sources can be very awkward when you are getting started because they can be hard to remember. They also may not sound very natural at first, but there are a few things to keep in mind.

Cites may come *before* the information. An example of a cite is listed below in bold:

According to a study conducted by Dr. Tina Cheng, director of pediatrics at the Johns Hopkins Children's Center, reported in the January 14, 2003 *New York Times*, nearly 70 percent of parents believe it is unacceptable for children to play with toy guns.

Yes, you would actually say all of that. It may sound long and difficult, especially to memorize, but it's important. Not all cites are that long, but good cites make a big difference. What if it didn't include Johns Hopkins Children's Center? What if it didn't include the fact that Tina Cheng is a doctor specializing in medical care for children? What if we didn't know that the research is current or that it was in a credible paper like the New York Times? This is a hard fact to believe on face value, but the cite makes it much more credible. And, yes, it is true. Look it up!

Cites should ALWAYS include the date and name of the publication or source being used. It might also include the name of the person who presented the information and information about their qualifications. It could also include information about where a study was conducted, the scope of the study and so on. In fact, you may have noticed that all citations in this textbook follow the same pattern your authors suggest!

Rule of Thumb: Give as much information as you deem necessary for people to understand and trust the information you are presenting. Common knowledge, such as the sky is blue, need not have cites. Quotations from others, facts, and specific information you read and include in your speech need to be documented, just as they must be in a research paper.

Source Citation Guidelines:

Cites must ALWAYS include:

The name of the publication, website, or person you interviewed
The date of publication, date the website was last updated, or the date of your interview

Cites often SHOULD include:

The credentials of the person who is cited
How the information was collected *(a study of 50 people)*
The author of the article or book, if relevant

Citation Language Suggestions:

"According to *publication* of *date*….."
"As reported in the *publication* of *date*….."
"On *date*, the *publication* reported that ….."
"The *publication* of *date* says that….."
"In a personal interview on *date*, with *title/name of person* …."
Or find language that is natural for you, but still complete and credible.

Conclusion

Ideas alone are not enough to sustain your speech. This chapter has shown you how you can develop your ideas by gathering outside resources and using them to clarify your ideas for the audience. We have covered the different places you may find research, supporting materials to identify and implement in your speech, and how to properly give credit to the sources you use. Earlier, we compared the research and support for your speech to muscles on a skeleton. Just as physical exercise is essential to build your muscles and keep them in shape, it is equally important that you exercise your research and analytical skills to find great support for every speech.

From Fright to MIGHT Moment

Worried about saying an important line "just right" in a speech? Consider borrowing someone else's words from an article, or even a poem or song. Just be sure to give credit to the author with a complete source citation.

Speakers' Secret

Whenever you are in a library and can't find the information you need, there is one person who can always help: THE REFERENCE LIBRARIAN.

He or she really is there to help you. If you need assistance, do not hesitate to ask.

Chapter 7 Terms & Concepts

Credibility
Cite
Comparison/contrast (Analogies)
Definition
Description
Examples
Expert testimony
Explanations
Factual example
Hypothetical example
Illustrations or Extended examples
Interview
Keyword search
Lay testimony
Personal Experience
Research
Source citation
Statistics
Support
Testimony
Web-based Research

Activity #1: Understanding Chapter 7

Answer the following items as true or false.
The answers appear in Appendix C.

1. Library research is required for every speech.	T	F
2. All cites must include the publication from which the information was taken.	T	F
3. Comparisons can be used to support an idea or argument.	T	F
4. Good research makes your speech more credible.	T	F
5. It is best to secretly tape record interviews so your subject won't get nervous.	T	F

ACTIVITY #2: Advantages and Disadvantages of Possible Sources

	ADVANTAGES	DISADVANTAGES
Your own experiences		
Books		
Magazines		
Journals/trade publications		
Newspapers		
TV/Radio programs		
Local and state agencies		
Internet sources		
Interviews		

Activity #3: Using Forms of Support

What could you say to **support** the idea presented using each *type* of support?

	"Chocolate chip cookies are the best cookies"	**"School violence is a serious problem."**
Descriptions	They are soft and gooey and warm and smell like chocolate and rich, sweet goodness.	
Definitions	The 1978 edition of *Cooking America* calls the chocolate chip cookie the "definitive American treat."	
Explanation or reasoning	If I ask you to think of a cookie, what kind pops into your head? Probably a chocolate chip cookie, because most of us consider it to be the standard among all cookies.	
Example (actual or hypothetical)	When I was 10, I skinned my knee on my bike. My Mom made me a batch of chocolate chip cookies, and they were so good I forgot all about the pain.	
Statistics and hard facts/data	According to *Hearty Eating* of May 1998, Americans eat more chocolate chip cookies than any other kind of cookie.	
Testimony	According to Mary Sample in her 1997 *Good Cookies Book*, "There is no cookie ever created that can match the quality of the classic chocolate chip. It's the best"	
Literal Comparison	While a sugar cookie may be good, a chocolate chip cookie has the extra punch of wonderful chocolate.	
Figurative Comparison	A chocolate chip cookie is the Ferrari of desserts.	
Visual/Audio aids	(Show a picture of a cookie being pulled apart with the chocolate chips stretching between the pieces.)	
Activities/ interactions with the audience	(Give out cookies for everyone to taste.)	

Activity #4: Research Interview

Plan and conduct a research **interview**. Follow these steps:

Step One: Brainstorm several possible people you could interview about your topic. Think big! Then select one or two people from the list to contact for an interview.

Step Two: Generate a list of interview questions:

- Try to ask open-ended questions, questions that require more than a yes or no answer.
- Always include questions about areas you don't understand even if they seem embarrassing.
- Always include the question, "Where else could I get more information about this topic?"

Step Three: Determine the best way to contact this person: a letter, phone call, or email.

- Contact the individual and request an appointment for an interview.
- Be ready with questions in case they say, "Right now!"
- Be gracious if they say no.
- Don't leave them long phone messages and ask them to PAGE you. Call back.
- Plan a time to meet with the person or call them for the interview.
- E-mailing back and forth is not as effective as a "live" interview, but can be effective if it's your only option. Recently, a student received e-mail responses to her interview questions from Christopher Reeve for a class speech about spinal injuries.

Step Four: Take very careful notes during the interview.

- Don't be afraid to ask your interviewee to repeat words or phrases that you didn't record the first time.
- You may even want to tape record the interview with a small, hand-held recorder, but always ask permission first. It is illegal to tape a phone conversation without the permission of the other person.
- As soon as the interview is over, go back through your notes and include information you didn't get down the first time.

Step Five: Always thank the interviewer at the conclusion of the interview and with a follow-up letter or note.

Developing and Ordering Main Points

Mr. Madison, what you've just said is one of the most insanely idiotic things I have ever heard. At no point in your rambling, incoherent response were you even close to anything that could be considered a rational thought. Every one in this room is now dumber for having listened to it. I award you no points, and may God have mercy on your soul. – Principal, *Billy Madison*

How is the specific purpose of your speech different than the general goal and central idea?

One of the things you learned in Chapter 5 was how to develop a specific purpose for a speech. In Chapter 7 you learned how to collect research about your topic. In this chapter we will discover how to combine this work to choose and organize the main points of your speech carefully.

There are three parts to every speech: the **introduction**, **body,** and **conclusion**. Each speech should begin with an **introduction** in which the central idea of your speech is revealed. Each speech should end with a **conclusion**, in which major aspects of the speech are reviewed. Your introduction usually comprises about 10% of the speech, and the conclusion about 5-10%. We will focus more on introductions and conclusions in Chapter 9.

Three Parts of Every Speech:

I. Introduction
II. Body
III. Conclusion

The majority of your speech is the **body**, the area in which you discuss each of your main points. It usually comprises 80-90% of the speech. Because of the amount of time spent on the body, careful development of this area is necessary.

Remember when you end a speech, most audience members won't be able to remember everything you said. With this in mind, speakers should provide structured main points that will be memorable.

Most speeches will have two or three main points, since audiences may have trouble remembering more than three ideas. This is just a rule of thumb, however. One speech student gave a wonderful speech about large families using twelve main points. Each main point represented one of her siblings! It was creative and effective. A few short ceremonial speeches may have only one main point in the speech. An example of this type of speech is a toast. Still, for most speeches, you will need to divide the body into at least two to three areas.

Developing Main Points

The best way to come up with main points for a speech is to review your specific purpose and then complete a seven-step process.

STEP ONE: Brainstorm a list of concepts that pertain to your specific purpose and/or relate to your topic.

Just as brainstorming was effective in selecting your topic, it can now be a great tool for generating an initial list of areas to cover in your speech. You should come up with at least 20 or 25 concepts and start a list.

STEP TWO: Review your research to add additional concepts to your list.

The books and articles you have collected should have additional information that is pertinent to your specific purpose. Summarize these concepts briefly and add them to your list.

STEP THREE: Ask yourself the journalist's questions to add additional concepts to your list.

Imagine you are a journalist writing a story about your topic. Ask yourself questions that begin with the following words:

Who?	**What?**	**When?**	**How much?**
Where?	**Why?**	**How?**	

If you don't already have items on your list that address these areas, add concepts to your list that answer these questions.

STEP FOUR: Use audience analysis to anticipate concepts your audience will expect to hear in your speech.

Imagine that you will be a member of the audience for your speech. Even better, speak with a few people who will be in the audience for your speech, such as your classmates. Identify areas in the realm of your specific purpose that will be of particular interest to that audience. Add these concepts to your list.

STEP FIVE: Reduce the list.

Keeping in mind your time limits and your specific purpose, remove some concepts from your list. You probably have several ideas that you generated which are redundant, too ambitious, or peripheral to your specific purpose and unnecessary.

STEP SIX: Group related concepts into 2-3 areas of commonality.

Number each item on your list with a 1, 2, or 3 based on similarities. These will become your main points. Come up with a label for each of your 2-3 main points that expresses what all the items have in common. Keep the list of ideas that fit into each area; these will be used later as subpoints when you write your outline.

STEP SEVEN: Improve your main point labels.

Carefully consider the way you phrase your main points since you will be saying each phrase many times during your speech. The language you choose must clearly explain what you will cover in that area and should also interest your audience.

For instance, in a speech about "Starting Your Own Garden," you might start out with a first point such as, "Things you do to get the ground ready for plants." You could make this clearer by changing it to, "Aerating your soil." It

Developing Main Points:

1. Brainstorm a list of concepts that pertain to your specific purpose.
2. Review your research to add additional concepts to your list.
3. Ask yourself the journalist's questions to add additional concepts to your list.
4. Use audience analysis to anticipate concepts your audience will expect to hear in your speech.
5. Reduce the list.
6. Group related concepts into 2-3 areas of commonality.
7. Improve your main point labels.

also might be more interesting to say, "Let's dig up some dirt on soil preparation."

Be sure to avoid the word "and" when you phrase a main point. If you use "and," then you really have two points. If this happens, either split the information into two different points or find another phrase that covers both concepts. For instance:

Before: "The history and early problems of airline construction"

After: "The challenging development of the first airplanes"

Main points should also be written in **parallel structure,** using similar structure or language in each label. For example, in her speech on African elephants, one student used the following main points:

I. African elephants are complicated.
II. African elephants are able to communicate.
III. African elephants are endangered.

Ordering Your Main Points

Your first consideration in ordering your points should be **logical** sequencing. For instance, in an informative explanation speech about "Understanding How a Car Engine Works," the following organization of points would be slightly illogical because it does not follow a logical progression:

I. The engine burns the fuel.
II. The exhaust system vents the engine.
III. The ignition system starts the car.

There are several ways to organize your speech logically, including the **Topical Sequence,** the **Chronological Sequence,** the **Spatial Sequence,** and the **Structure-Function Sequence.**

THE TOPICAL SEQUENCE

In the **topical sequence,** points are ordered based on the logical divisions of the topic. They are categorical in nature. These categories or divisions are the subdividing of the topic into different parts. The topical organizational pattern is the most often used organization for speeches. It is the most used because most topics can be organized by subdividing the topic into different parts.

Consider the following topical sequence for a speech about the accomplishments of Ronald Reagan.

I. **Ronald Reagan accomplished a great deal as an actor.**
II. **Ronald Reagan accomplished a great deal as Governor of California.**
III. **Ronal Reagan accomplished a great deal as President of the United States.**

THE CHRONOLOGICAL SEQUENCE

In the **chronological sequence,** points are ordered based on linear time from earliest to latest, first to last. Consider the following chronological main points for a speech about making a cake.

I. **The first step is to mix the ingredients.**
II. **The second step is to bake the cake.**
III. **The third step is to decorate the cake.**

The chronological sequence can also be used to discuss a topic as viewed over a period of time.

I. **Baseball was invented as a simple game.**
II. **Baseball had a period called "The glory days."**
III. **Baseball is a high profit business.**

A very simple chronological structure is to discuss the past, present, and future of a topic.

I. **Historically, women played an important role in politics.**
II. **Today, women are in many places of leadership.**
III. **In the future, a woman will be elected president.**

THE SPATIAL SEQUENCE

In the **spatial sequence**, points are ordered based on physical location. This may include special orientation from east to west, top to bottom, or left to right. These geographical or directional patterns help the audience to clearly see a "movement" from point to point as the speech unfolds.

The following is an example of a spatial sequence organizational pattern.

I. **The core of the earth is in the center of the sphere.**
II. **The earth's mantle is the next layer outward from the center.**
III. **The crust of the earth is on the outside of the sphere.**

THE STRUCTURE-FUNCTION SEQUENCE

Finally, in the **structure-function sequence** points are ordered in a fashion to describe something and then show how it works. It is usually organized in 2 or 3 main points.

The following is an example of a structure-function organizational pattern discussing the workings of a computer:

I. **The components of the computer hard drive**
II. **How the hard drive stores files**
III. **How information is accessed from the hard drive**

In addition to logical sequencing, another consideration in ordering your points is how *interesting* your main points will be to your audience. A general guideline is to begin with a point that will get your audience involved while saving the most interesting point for last. In a three-point speech, it would look like this:

I. **Second most interesting point**
II. **Least interesting point**
III. **Most interesting point**

Additional speech structures will be described in Chapter 15, Persuasive Speaking.

Conclusion

The development of main points provides the overall blueprint for a speech. If you take the time to carefully and thoughtfully complete this process, you will already have a thorough and ordered list of all the concepts your speech will include, including your sub-points. The next step is to formalize your organization and flesh out the body of your speech with your outline, as described in Chapter 10.

FROM FRIGHT TO MIGHT MOMENT

An audience may tune you out if they can't follow your speech's organization. Making sure that you have clear and interesting main points will give you the confidence of knowing that your audience wants to listen.

Tough Crowd?

If you know (based on audience analysis) you will be speaking to a crowd that may be averse to hearing what you have to say, consider the following order for your points:

I. **The point the audience will agree with most**
II. **The point the audience will agree with next most**
III. **The most controversial point**

Chapter 8: Terms & Concepts

Body
Chronological Sequence
Conclusion
Coordinate Ideas
Introduction
Logical Sequence
Main Points
Organizational Pattern
Parallel Structure
Spatial Sequence
Structure-Function Sequence
Subordinate Ideas
Topical Sequence

Activity #1: Understanding Chapter 8

Answer the following items as true or false.
Answers appear in Appendix C.

1. You should almost always start your speech with your most interesting main point.	T	F
2. Most speeches have four main points.	T	F
3. The chronological sequence is related to space.	T	F
4. Your main points should be written in parallel structure.	T	F
5. Tropical sequencing is a legitimate organizational pattern.	T	F

Activity #2: Developing Main Points

Develop main points for each of the following topics. Be sure to carefully phrase and order the points.

1. **An informative speech about "Your Favorite Places to Eat Out"** using the spatial sequence.

2. **A memorable experience speech about "Bad Hairstyles"** using the topical sequence.

3. **An informative speech about "The Sinking of the Titanic"** using the chronological sequence.

Introductions, Conclusions, and Transitions

I am the beginning and the end. I bring order into chaos. –Borg Queen, *Star Trek; First Contact*

After you have developed the body of your speech, it is time to focus on the first and last parts of your speech, your introduction and conclusion, and on the flow of ideas between your main points, your transitions.

Introductions

Introductions do not include a lot of information about the topic of your speech. That information should be presented in the body of the speech. However, introductions do achieve six important goals.

> **Goals of an Introduction:**
>
> - Get the audience's *attention*
> - Clearly *reveal* the speech topic
> - Generate *interest* in the topic/show its significance to the audience
> - Provide a *preview* or "road map"
> - Create *rapport*
> - Demonstrate your personal *credibility*

First, introductions must **gain the attention** of the audience so they will be ready to hear the material to follow.

Second, introductions must clearly **reveal your speech topic** to your audience.

Third, introductions need to **get your audience interested in your topic** so they care enough to listen to the rest of the speech.

Fourth, introductions should give a **preview** or **"road map"** to the audience so they know where the speech is going. Specifically, this means telling them what your main points will be.

Fifth, introductions should **create rapport**. Rapport is a friendly feeling between you and your audience so they will be open and receptive to what you have to say, even if they initially disagree with your position.

Sixth, you must **establish your personal credibility** in your introduction so the audience believes what you will say in the rest of the speech.

There are four content areas you should cover in every introduction to make sure you achieve these goals. These are the attention device, topic revelation statement, significance statement, and a preview of the main points.

THE ATTENTION DEVICE

The **attention device** is designed to gain the attention of the audience. You want the audience to listen. Let us discuss several possible devices you may use to gain the attention of the audience.

Ask a rhetorical question. This question may be real or hypothetical. "Do you ever wake up in the middle of the night and hear children crying? Sandy was one child that cried herself to sleep each night because she was beaten routinely." While this example is real, you may want to use a hypothetical example. "Can you imagine yourself waking up in the middle of the night crying because you've been beaten by your parents?"

Use a provocative or stimulating statement. "Despite what you have heard, humans have never walked on the moon. It was all an elaborate hoax."

Refer to a recent event. "Two weeks ago classes at this college were cancelled because of severe weather conditions, resulting in over 150 deaths. Today, I would like to talk about the life of the tornado."

Begin with humor. Tell a joke. Humor is a very effective way to begin a speech, as long as you avoid potentially offensive jokes and relate the joke to your topic revelation statement.

Make a reference to the audience. "It is a pleasure to be speaking before such a well educated group of individuals. My research indicates that more of this community college faculty has earned doctoral degrees than the average at four year universities in California."

Make a reference to the occasion. "As a former member of this school's track team, I am especially honored to be invited back to deliver a speech at the dedication of this new stadium."

Begin with a quotation. "As Mark Twain once said, 'We should never let school get in the way of education'." When you use a quotation, it is important to link the quotation to your topic revelation statement.

Begin with a hypothetical situation. "Today, take a vacation from your everyday existence. You are a student at the most prestigious college in the United States. You are attending this college because you have earned enough scholarship money to pay for your entire tuition, room, board, and even extra spending money. Do you like this college experience?"

Begin with a story. It can be about someone else or yourself. "Janine Jeffrey was only 20 years old. She carried 23 units each semester of her college life, always attended summer school, and completed her master's degree in nine months. Her friends called her an overachiever." A technique many speakers employ with this device is to save the ending of the story for the lasting thought in the conclusion of the speech.

Begin with a startling statistic. "More than 2,000 people desiring to become immigrants in Europe have been denied entry into European countries since 1993. This June 19, 2000 statistic from *Reuters* points out the extreme plight of immigrants."

You may also use, an illustration, an analogy, an example from popular culture, a historical anecdote, a political anecdote, a role-play, or audio or visual aid in addition to the devices listed above. In fact, there are countless types of possible attention devices. The key is to use your imagination. Never just begin a speech with, "Hi, my name is ______ and my topic is ______."

THE TOPIC REVELATION STATEMENT

The second area needed for an outstanding introduction is the identification of your **topic revelation statement.** Remember from Chapter 5 that this is the sentence where you clearly present your topic to the audience.

THE SIGNIFICANCE STATEMENT

The third area needed for an outstanding introduction is a **significance statement.** Significance refers to the way in which the topic is important to the audience and why it is important to you as a speaker. Whenever possible, use a source citation to build your significance. Testimony from a credible person in the field of your topic is frequently used to demonstrate significance. At a minimum, a significance statement must plainly state why the audience should keep listening to the remainder of your speech.

PREVIEW OF MAIN POINTS

The fourth and final area needed for an outstanding introduction is the **preview of main points.** The preview statement lists your main points in the same order they will occur in the body of the speech.

If you have selected and thoughtfully labeled your main points, constructing your preview is easy. Simply provide an order indicator then state your first point label, give another order indicator and state your second point label, then an order indicator and your third point label, and so on for each main point. Order indicators are sequenced words like, "First, second, and third," or "First, next, and last."

An example of a preview statement is:

> **"First, I'll discuss two important historical aspects of golf, second, two heroes of golf, and third, the six most important rules of golf."**

Sample Introduction:

Attention Device: The ingredients in a hot dog. Nobody really likes to talk about them, but we all know what they are: leftover pig parts, right? Actually, somebody had a great idea. Instead of throwing away the leftover parts after the roasts and ribs have been used, let's do something useful -- even profitable -- with them. And it worked. Well, the pork industry isn't the only industry to show some creative use of leftovers. Now the garment industry is doing the same thing with their biggest leftover.

Topic Revelation Statement: In the next few minutes, I will reveal to you the surprising capabilities of those annoying fuzz balls we call "lint."

Significance Statement: Sure, lint may seem insignificant, even irritating, but *Scientific American* of August 1997 reports that it may soon be used in building our homes, paving our roads, and it might even end up on the dinner table!

Preview of Main Points: First I will explain the characteristics of industrial lint. Next, I'll show you how it's being used in construction, and, finally, I'll tempt your taste buds with some possible lint lunches of the future.

Additionally, your nonverbal communication style must also work to achieve the goals of an introduction. Your energy level and eye contact can help create attention and interest. Your rate and articulation will help the audience clearly understand your topic. Your facial expressions, voice, and appearance will also create positive rapport and credibility.

Conclusions

Conclusions of speeches are also important because they leave the audience with a final summary and impression of your entire presentation. Conclusions are generally not as long as introductions but have two important goals. These goals are the two content aspects of the conclusion.

The first goal of the conclusion is to **review the topic statement and main points** of your speech. Reiterate what your purpose was or what you wanted to accomplish in giving the speech, and the main points you used to achieve your goal. When you summarize, the audience will be more likely to remember these concepts after your speech has ended.

Goals of a Conclusion:

- Clearly *review* the speech topic and main points
- Create a powerful lasting thought in the mind of each audience member

The second goal of the conclusion is to create a **lasting thought** about your speech. This is achieved by sharing an idea or phrase that brings the concepts of the speech together and will remain with the audience after your speech has ended. A good way to create psychological unity for the audience is to tie-in your lasting thought with the attention device you used in the introduction. This is easily done when you return and complete a story you used in the opening of the speech. You may also choose to end with a meaningful quotation, a final call for action, or your personal feelings about the topic you discussed.

Remember from Chapter 3 to "End Strong." Never end with a weak phrase or a cliché like, "thank you" or "that's about it." The last line and last word should be powerful, vivid, and memorable. Think of it as the final note at the end of a symphony. It must also be delivered well. You want to allow the speech to resonate well beyond the moment you leave the stage. Always hold the last moment before you walk away from the speaking situation and walk back to your seat with confidence and poise.

Sample Conclusion:

Review of Topic and Main Points: Today we have discussed the surprising new uses of lint. We learned its composition, uses in construction, and even its nutritional possibilities.

Lasting Thought: It took innovation and a little courage for the first person to try a hot dog, but what an innovation it was! What would a trip to a baseball game be without them? Perhaps soon, even though it will seem a little unusual, you may hear the vendor at the game yelling, "Get your pretzels, get your hot dogs, get your lint burgers!"

Transitions

Transitions are the phrases used to connect the major parts of your speech together. Think of them as bridges. Bridges allow us to get from one point to the next without falling into water or down a path we don't want to travel. The transition allows us to go from one point of the speech to the next without getting lost. In a three-point speech, you will have four distinct transition statements:

INTRODUCTION to **FIRST MAIN POINT**
FIRST MAIN POINT to **SECOND MAIN POINT**
SECOND MAIN POINT to **THIRD MAIN POINT**
THIRD MAIN POINT to **CONCLUSION**

The transition immediately following your introduction is a simple transition. It alerts the audience to your arrival at the first point:

"So let's find out about the ingredients you'll need for your cake."

The remaining transitions should be **summary transitions** which review the previous main point and carry the audience into the next point. For instance, a transition from the first point to the second point might be:

"Now that you know the ingredients you need, I will explain how to make your batter."

Even though they may sound repetitive and obvious to you, clear transitions are necessary signposts for your audience. Listening comprehension is far worse than reading comprehension, so we need to make every possible effort to keep the audience from being lost and confused during our speeches.

Conclusion

Although introductions, transitions, and conclusions contain relatively little information about your speech topic, they are still vital components to the overall effectiveness of your speech. Take some time to prepare and practice these critical elements of your speech.

From FRIGHT to MIGHT Moment

If you feel nervous about delivering your speech, take the time to memorize the first line of your introduction and the last line of your conclusion. In addition to reducing some of your anxiety, it will make your speech delivery even more effective!

Speakers' Secret

Studies into theories about the beginning and ending of a message (known as the *primacy* and *recency effects*) show that both areas have a strong impact in the overall perception of a message.

You can take advantage of this knowledge by spending extra time creating your introduction and conclusion and then rehearsing their delivery over and over for the best possible primacy and recency effect!

Chapter 9: Terms & Concepts:

Attention device
Conclusion
Credibility
Humor
Hypothetical situation
Introduction
Lasting thought
Preview
Quotation
Rapport
Rhetorical question
Road map
Significance statement
Startling statistic
Stimulating statement
Summary
Transitions

ACTIVITY #1: Understanding Chapter 9

Answer the following items as true or false.
Answers appear in Appendix C.

1. Introductions should include a lot of detailed information about your topic area.	T	F
2. You should include your specific purpose in your introduction.	T	F
3. There are four content areas to cover in a conclusion.	T	F
4. The preview statement lists your main points in the same order they will occur in the body of the speech.	T	F
5. Transitions are the phrases used to connect the major parts of your speech together.	T	F

Activity #2: Write an Introduction

Attention device:__________________________________

Topic revelation statement: ___________________________

Significance statement (use a *source citation*): ______________

Preview of main points:________________________________

Now, explain how you will achieve the goals of *rapport* and *personal credibility* during your introduction: ______________________

Activity #3: Attention Devices

Work alone or with a partner to come up with possible attention devices for the following two topics in each of the categories given.

Attention Device Category	Topic #1: How to play basketball	Topic #2: Racial profiling by the police
Rhetorical question		
Provocative or stimulating statement		
Reference to a recent event		
Humor		
Quotation		
Startling statistic		
Real-life story		
Hypothetical scenario		
Historical anecdote		
Pop culture example		

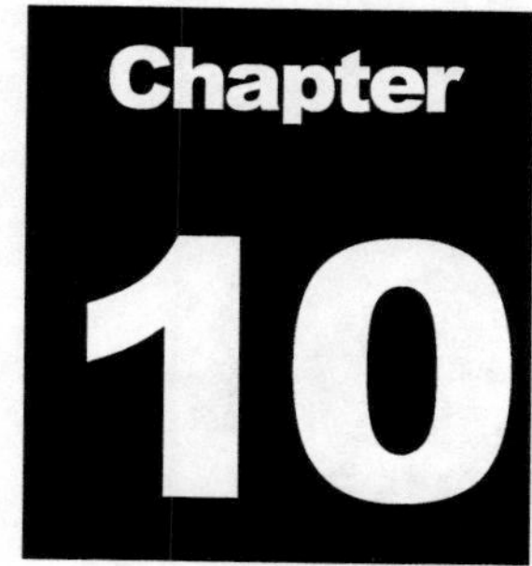

Outlining

Woo-hoo! Who would've guessed that reading and writing would pay off? - Homer Simpson, *The Simpsons*

What other classes have required you to produce outlines?

Most important undertakings begin with some type of plan. Before the Sears Tower was erected in Chicago, architects and designers spent several years drafting the blueprints to ensure that the actual building process went smoothly. Just like the Sears Tower, each speech in this class needs careful design and planning well before your first performance. A crucial step in this planning process is creating an outline. Outlining is important for three reasons.

THE FIRST FUNCTION OF AN OUTLINE

The first function of an outline is **to help you organize the speech** into appropriate main points and subpoints. **Main points** are identified in the outline by Roman numerals. This is a visual cue for the speaker that the speech topic has equal subdivisions. Subordinate Ideas are the **Subpoints** that develop and clarify the main points. They are identified by capital letters, such as A, B, C. If any of the subpoints need further development, create sub-subpoints, and so on.

Sub-subpoints, identified by numbers, 1,2,3 and **Sub-sub-subpoints,** identified by a,b,c, are used.

I. Main point
- **A. Subpoint**
- **B. Subpoint**
  - **1. Sub-subpoint**
  - **2. Sub-subpoint**
    - **a. Sub-sub-subpoint**
    - **b. Sub-sub-subpoint**

II. **Main point**
   - A. **Subpoint**
   - B. **Subpoint**
     1. **Sub-subpoint**
     2. **Sub-subpoint**
   - C. **Subpoint**

THE SECOND FUNCTION OF AN OUTLINE

The second function of an outline is **to ensure your speech has a logical sequence.** The main points need to be developed rationally.

To ensure your outline follows a logical pattern and fully incorporates all of your research, adhere to the following principles when organizing your main points, subpoints, sub-subpoints, and beyond.

Functions of an Outline:

- To help you organize the speech
- To ensure that your speech has a logical progression
- To help you practice and deliver the speech

Simplicity is the first principle of outlining. This means that each symbol of the outline should be followed by only one idea or statement. You must make your ideas easy to follow. The whole reason for crafting an outline is to show the logical division of ideas and support you have. If ideas are not split up into the smallest possible units, you defeat the purpose of writing an outline. Be aware this may mean dividing and subdividing the information contained in a source. The example below illustrates how an idea can be divided into simpler units.

I. **In order to develop proper study habits, you should create a good study space, get plenty of rest, and organize your study materials.**

This main point has three different ideas. It should be divided so each line contains only one idea.

I. **There are several steps to developing proper study habits.**

   A. **You should create a good study space.**

   B. **You should get plenty of rest.**

   C. **You should organize your study materials.**

Subordination is the second principle of outlining. Splitting information into A-B-C or 1-2-3 is easy, but subordination requires each idea in your outline support the idea that is superior to it symbolically. In other words, each subpoint must directly support the main point under which it falls. Each sub-subpoint must support the subpoint under which it falls. This example demonstrates a subpoint that does not support its main point.

I. A lawn mower has many uses.

- **A. It cuts grass.**
- **B. It provides exercise to the person mowing.**
- **C. There are several maintenance concerns with a lawnmower.**
  - **1. Adjustments must be made to the motor.**
  - **2. The blade must be sharpened.**
  - **3. The engine must be properly lubricated.**
  - **4. The mower must be properly stored.**

The problem with this organization is that the maintenance concerns have nothing to do with the uses of a lawn mower. Let's make the maintenance concerns a separate main point.

I. A lawn mower has many uses.

- **A. It cuts grass.**
- **B. It provides exercise to the person mowing.**

II. There are several maintenance concerns with a lawnmower.

- **A. Adjustments must be made to the motor.**
- **B. The blade must be sharpened.**
- **C. The engine must be properly lubricated.**
- **D. The mower must be properly stored.**

Finally, let's look at one more example from an actual student speech to see both principles of simplicity and subordination in action.

I. Married women should not be allowed to work for pay because their husbands support them and many of them have inheritances. Besides, unemployed men and un-married women need these jobs, and married women let their outside work interfere with their duties at home.

To simplify this idea, we should identify the *main point.* It should stand by itself:

I. Married women should not be allowed to work for pay.

The information after this idea supports it, so it should be *subordinate.* One option would be to structure the outline in this way:

I. Married women should not be allowed to work for pay.

A. Their husbands support them.

B. Many of them have inheritances.

C. Unemployed men need these jobs.

D. Un-married women need these jobs.

E. They let their outside work interfere with their duties at home.

This organization is not the best, though, for two reasons. First, ideas repeat themselves (e.g., "_____ need these jobs."). Second, there are no sub-subpoints. Not every idea in your outline is of equal importance. Only *major ideas* should be classified as subpoints. Consider this reorganization:

I. Married women should not be allowed to work for pay.

A. They do not need to earn money.

1. Their husbands support them.

2. Many of them have inheritances.

B. Their jobs are needed by others.

1. Some men are unemployed.

2. Many un-married women need to support themselves.

C. Outside work interferes with their home duties.

Notice that this organization includes two ideas that were not in the original paragraph. ("They do not need to earn money" and "Their jobs are needed by others") Sometimes a little creativity and analysis are required to take some pieces of information and link them together. Here, two different examples – support from husbands and inheritance – were used correctly as *supporting materials* for a brand new idea created by the speaker.

THE THIRD FUNCTION OF AN OUTLINE

The third function of an outline is **to help the speaker practice and deliver the speech.** Classroom speeches are often extemporaneous, meaning the speaker prepares the complete content of the speech including a very thorough outline but does not write the speech out word for word. The outline helps the speaker practice because the main points are clearly identified by the Roman numerals. For instance, to find the next main point, you only have to look down at the outline to the next Roman numeral.

You will learn that there are three kinds of outlines for every speech that you will give. One is designed as you prepare your materials. One is to be given to the professor. The last outline is the one you will use when delivering the speech.

The Working Outline

The first stage of outlining should begin with a working outline, developed as you decide the organizational structure of your speech. Once you have gathered all of your research, start creating a list of all the ideas, facts, stories, quotations, statistics, and general information you wish to cover about a topic. After you have created this list, group and rearrange ideas into some type of logical pattern.

A working outline is a rough draft of the main ideas and subpoints of your speech. This working outline will go through many drafts and changes before your ideas are finalized.

As you develop your main points and subpoints, you will want to keep in mind the ideas of simplicity and balance. Since most speeches you give in class will be less than ten minutes, too many subpoints or sub-subpoints will likely lead you to exceed your time limit or have to cut information after your speech is drafted. Also, strive to balance the information contained in each point. An outline that has six subpoints for Main Point #1, but only two for Main Point #2, is weighted too heavily towards one idea. If this is the case, consider eliminating subpoints or seeing if several of them could be reorganized into another main point.

The Formal Outline

Once you have made the final decisions about the organization of your speech, you are ready to create a formal outline. A formal outline reflects your finished product and the exact points you will cover. It will allow you to look at your speech as a whole and to make sure the ideas flow logically together. The formal outline should contain enough information so someone who missed your speech could review your formal outline and have a very good understanding of exactly what you covered. It is the *formal document* of your speech. Your instructor may require that this formal outline meet the following standards:

The parts of the speech are labeled (Introduction, Body, Conclusion). Separating the parts of your speech will make it easier for someone reading your outline to see where each begins and ends. Additionally, it will benefit you by forcing you to completely develop each part of your introduction, body, and conclusion.

It is written in complete sentences. While key words and phrases are fine for a working outline, *all* ideas in your formal outline should be expressed in complete sentences. Since this is a document of your speech, and the final stage of your preparation, all ideas need to be complete so you have the best idea of what you want to say. Complete sentences will also make it easier for you to integrate testimony, statistics, and sources into your speech.

It contains your specific purpose and topic revelation statement. You need to identify these while preparing a speech, but they can also serve an important function in your outline. Double check all information in your outline, and make sure it meets the goals set forth in your specific purpose and topic revelation statement.

It uses a formalized pattern of symbols to outline ideas. To check for effective use of the principles of outlining, it is best to use a standard pattern of outline symbols. Refer to the beginning of the chapter for the most commonly used symbols. Also remember it is impossible to divide an idea into only one part. Therefore, if you have an "A" subpoint, you <u>must</u> have a "B" subpoint to complete the division of the idea. The same holds true for "1" and "2" sub-subpoints and "a" and "b" sub-sub-subpoints. If you find you only have one sub-subpoint for an idea, consider how you can either create another sub-subpoint to go with it, or integrate that sub-subpoint into the subpoint it supports.

It contains a bibliography or "Works Cited" page. It is important to give proper credit to your sources. A formalized bibliography provides a context for the sources you will cite in your speech and makes it easy for someone who wants to learn more about your topic to find some excellent resources. Your instructor may require you to use the guidelines of the Modern Language Association (MLA), American Psychological Association (APA), or another format. Ask your instructor for assistance if you do not know how to construct a formal bibliography. A brief guide to MLA and APA citation can be found in Appendix C.

It is typed. Make sure you proofread your typed outline for proper formatting, punctuation, spelling, and grammar. Do not rely on your word processing program to catch every mistake. Read the document yourself.

The Speaking Outline

Finally, you will create some speaking notes to aid in your delivery. These notes are referred to as a speaking outline. For most instructors, the speaking outline must fit on a few notecards. Given this size constraint, here are some guidelines for creating a speaking outline:

1. **Express ideas in key words.**

2. **Write or type clearly and legibly and large enough to read.**

3. **Use a consistent pattern.**

4. **Limit the information as much as possible.**

One helpful tip for creating your speaking outline is *never* shrink your formal outline down to a tiny font and paste it on your note cards. This is a recipe for disaster. You don't need your entire formal outline in front of you to give the speech. Additionally, it will increase your temptation to read directly from your notes and eliminate eye contact with your audience. Few if any speakers can read very small text, so your notes will be largely useless!

If you are having trouble figuring out what to write on your notes, one suggestion is to practice delivering your speech without any notes. Naturally, you will forget information and leave out parts of your speech, but now you will know what you need on your notes to remind you. Things you are likely to forget, which should almost always be on your speaking outline, include dates, statistics, testimony, and source citations.

Finally, use your notes to write **delivery cues.** Whether you are speaking from a manuscript or extemporaneously from note cards, it is unlikely your audience will see your notes. Therefore, you can write reminders to yourself to smile or make eye contact. You can also indicate places to pause or directions on how to use your voice in a certain spot. Make your notes not just a reference for information, but a complete guide to help you give the best speech you can.

As you work on your outline, keep in mind your instructor will have different expectations about outlining than may be presented here. Listen carefully for the instructions for each of your assignments.

Conclusion

In this chapter we have explained the importance of outlining as well as how to structure your speech. This included the functions of an outline, the principles of outlining, and the various types of outlines. Stay organized.

From FRIGHT to MIGHT Moment

Use your speaking outline to boost your confidence while delivering a speech. In addition to delivery cues, write a note reminding you to speak for the audience or to project confidence in your voice.

Speakers' Secret

Be careful when typing your outline on a word processing program, especially Microsoft Word.

The auto-outlining function can really make a mess of things fast if you aren't an expert at using it. It may be a good idea to turn off auto formatting while you create your outline to avoid hours of hassle!

Chapter 10: Terms & Concepts

Coding	Notes
Delivery Cues	Simplicity
Formal outline	Speaking outline
Logical pattern	Subordination
Main point	Subpoint

Activity #1: Understanding Chapter 10

Answer the following items as true or false.
Answers appear in Appendix C.

1. Outlining helps you organize a speech.	T	F
2. Formal outlines should be expressed in key words, not complete sentences.	T	F
3. Formal outlines should always be typed.	T	F
4. Speaking outlines should be expressed in full sentences.	T	F
5. You should have limited notes on your note card during your speech.	T	F

Activity #2: Constructing a Formal Outline

1. Below is a main point from a student persuasive speech. Practice your outlining skills by condensing this paragraph into a full-sentence, formal outline.

2. Now go a step further and condense this full-sentence outline into a keyword, speaking outline.

Air Safety Week of August 18th, 1997, published results of a three year study involving in flight accidents and found that 99% involved pieces of carry on luggage falling out and hitting passengers or crew. The most common source of injuries were briefcases. One passenger was injured by a briefcase containing 40 rolls of quarters. Almost a dozen were hit by laptop computers in cases. Among the unlikely items people choose to carry on are fax machines, camcorders, coolers, strollers, televisions, rice cookers, stereo systems, and even bowling balls. *Newsday* of December 30th, 1997, argues that carry-on luggage can become missiles during turbulence. Even if they don't hit you, the *Sacramento Bee* of Jan 4th, 1998 says they sometimes block exits in emergency situations, and if you have to climb over bags to exit a burning aircraft you might not get out alive.

Language

I don't swear for the hell of it. Language is a poor enough means of communication. We've got to use all the words we've got. Besides, there are damn few words anybody understands. -Drummond, *Inherit the Wind*

Musician Gloria Estefan once sang a song called "The Words Get in the Way." She was singing about expressing feelings of love. Sometimes the words also get in the way when writing or delivering a speech.

Posit the following inquiry: How do you feel when speakers use words that you don't understand?

Some speakers use language that is above the heads of the audience (or their own), while others may use language that is inaccurate, vague, or inappropriate. In all of these cases, the words the speakers choose get in the way of the message they are trying to send with their speech. In many cases, the ineffective use of language can also lead an audience to conclude that a speaker is unintelligent, unprofessional, untrustworthy, or uninformed about their topic area. For these reasons, it is vital that you address the issue of language in your speech preparation.

In some speech situations (manuscript and memorized speeches) you will have the opportunity to sculpt every word for the best effect. Language matters in extemporaneous and impromptu speeches, too! Because of this, truly great speakers work to improve their use of language all the time so that they can be just as effective with language when unprepared speaking situations arise.

Improving Your Language Choices

None of us are born speaking a language. All language is learned. Unfortunately, students of today do not seem to be learning vocabulary as students once did. In his book *The Inarticulate Society,* Tom Schachtman quoted a CNN report that the average fourteen-year-old in 1996 had a vocabulary of 10,000 words while the average fourteen-year-old in 1950 had a vocabulary of 25,000 words. That means the student of today would have to learn an additional 15,000 words to have similar vocabulary skills as the student of 1950.

Schachtman goes on to remind us that "articulate behavior is the product of learning." We talk a lot, he says, but we are rarely eloquent. Eloquence is important as it goes hand in hand with a healthy democracy. Success depends upon using the language well.

When speaking, work to make sure your language, is **clear**. This will allow the listeners to understand the message. Make sure the language is also vivid, so it impacts the audience emotionally.

CLARITY IN LANGUAGE

Above all, we must be understood immediately when we speak. **Clarity** refers to the accuracy with which an audience understands a speaker's intended meaning. Listeners don't have time to look up words they don't comprehend.. There are six simple steps to help you achieve clarity in your choice of speaking language: choose familiar words, use concrete words, be accurate, be specific, be concise and avoid junk words.

Six Ways to Ensure Clarity:

- Choose familiar words.
- Use concrete words.
- Be accurate.
- Be specific.
- Be concise.
- Avoid junk words.

Choose familiar words. Familiar words are words well known to the audience. Consider such things as background, interests, and educational level. You may have words in your vocabulary that are not in all other people's vocabularies -- words that come from your job, hobbies, or sports you play. Such professional terminology is called **jargon**. Similarly, words used in casual conversation with meanings specific to a limited group of people are called **slang**.

The **multiple meanings** of words cause problems for the public speaker. Many words have a number of meanings. The speaker chooses the words assuming the audience will understand. However, some audience members may think of one of the other meanings of the word and thus be confused. For example, the word "fly" has different meanings to a pilot, a baseball player, a rap musician, and a tailor. If you use a word such as "fly" in a speech, you may have to define it.

Use concrete words. Concrete words are specific, refer to practical objects, and are not abstract or ambiguous. **Abstract words** are words that are general, broad, and refer to ideas or concepts. The more abstract the word, the more room for misinterpretation because the words are far removed from the object. **The Ladder of Abstraction** lists words that refer to the same thing from abstract to concrete.

The Ladder of Abstraction:

Human being

Adult human

Woman

Instructor

Speech instructor

Professor Colleen Tan

You should avoid ambiguity whenever possible. **Ambiguity** leaves your ideas open to various interpretations. For example, if you ask five people to envision what they understand the word "melon" to mean, you will get five different answers. However, if you use the more concrete term "watermelon," the five people will likely imagine very similar things. You have eliminated some of the ambiguity.

Be accurate. Accurate language refers to the correct meaning and usage of a word. If you are unsure of the correct meaning and usage of a word, *look it up*. Nothing is more embarrassing or more likely to undermine your credibility than misusing a word or making up a word that doesn't exist.

For example, what's wrong with the following sentence?

> **Irregardless of the situation, these two nations will never be friendly. Their amity goes back centuries.**

If you can't find two clear accuracy errors, you'd better identify the words you don't know and *look them up*!

Be specific. There are words that are *vague* and words that are *specific.* Vague words describe many possible things, while **specific words** only refer to one or a few things. Commonly used vague words and phrases include: *stuff*, *a bunch*, *like*, *things*, *sort of*, and *fine* (as in "I feel fine.").

For example, the sentence "A *great many* people left the community in 1997," is not as compelling as, "Sixty-five percent of residents left the community in 1997."

Being specific is particularly important in persuasive speeches where you are trying to influence attitudes and behavior. Which of the following sales pitches would you be more likely to act upon?

Vague: Come on <u>down here soon</u> and get some <u>stuff</u> and we'll give you <u>a deal.</u>

Specific: Come to <u>any Circuit Castle</u> <u>before midnight tonight</u> and we'll give you <u>20% off the current sale price</u> on <u>all televisions.</u>

Be concise. Concise language refers to using a limited number of words that are not repeated and trimming the fat from the speech. If you choose words that are familiar, concrete, and specific you won't need a lot of them. More words do not mean something is better. In fact, the box to the left reveals that some of the most important documents or speeches in history are very concise.

Word Counts:

Pythagorean Theorem: 24 words

The Lord's Prayer: 66 words

Archimedes' Principle: 67 words

The Ten Commandments: 179 words

The Gettysburg Address: 286 words

The Declaration of Independence: 1,300 words

Government regulations on the sale of cabbage: 26,911 words

VIVIDNESS IN LANGUAGE

Being understood is great, but you want your message to be remembered. You also want to inspire your audience's imaginations and senses so what you say will stick. **Vivid language** refers to lively language that makes an impact on the audience emotionally because of interest, energy, and images. It gets the audience involved.

Avoid Cliches. A **cliché** is a worn out expression; a stale or trite remark. The first person who said, "It's raining cats and dogs" came up with a great image. But, when you hear it now, do you actually imagine cats and dogs falling from the sky? Probably not, which is why the phrase is a cliché.

Use descriptive imagery. There are two types of imagery you can use: *literal* and *figurative.*

> **Literal imagery** is the use of words or phrases that trigger images in your listener's mind via direct description. For example, the sentence "I ate a steak for dinner" is clear. The sentence, 'I ate a thick, sizzling, smothered-in-mushrooms, melt-in-your-mouth steak" is memorable.
>
> **Figurative imagery** involves the use of similes and metaphors. You may recall from an English class that a **simile** is an explicit comparison of two unlike things, using the phrase "like" or "as" in

the comparison ("fresh as a daisy"). A **metaphor** is an implied comparison of two things that seem dissimilar, usually to relate an abstract concept to something more concrete ("The heart is a lonely hunter").

Use rhythm. Just like a great song, a great sentence has an effective rhythm. **Rhythm** refers to the arrangement of words to create certain effects. There are several ways to create rhythm using language.

Four Ways to Ensure Vividness:

- Avoid cliches.
- Use descriptive imagery.
- Use rhythm.
- Personalize.

Repetition: Repeat a phrase to reinforce a point. Representative Richard Gephardt used this technique during the Clinton impeachment hearings in the US House of Representatives when he said, "Let all of us here today say 'no' to resignation, 'no' to impeachment, 'no' to hatred, 'no' to intolerance of each other, and 'no' to vicious self-righteousness."

Parallelism: Arrange a series of words or phrases into a similar pattern. "I came, I saw, I conquered."

Alliteration: Repeat the same first consonant sound in a series of words. "Today's lesson will stress confidence, competence and compassion."

Antithesis: Contrast two ideas in a parallel structure and suggest there is a choice to be made. "Ask not what your country can do for you, ask what you can do for your country." (John F. Kennedy)

Personalize. Get your listeners involved by using words and phrases that hit home, such as the personal pronouns like *you*, *yours*, and *ours*. When possible, replace the words *people* (us), *the United States* (our country), and *college students* (students like us).

For example, "Thirty-three percent of Californians will be affected by cancer" is not as personal as "One out of every three people you know will be affected by cancer."

Appropriate Language

In the film "South Park: Bigger, Longer, and Uncut" there is a major national controversy about the use of inappropriate language by children. The kids in the film have an understanding about what they find appropriate, and their parents have a very different opinion. Similarly, audiences responded differently to the language in the film itself. Some found the swearing, sexual references, and shocking terminology to be hilarious; others walked out of the theater.

Appropriate Language varies from audience to audience because it refers to language that is right, suitable, and proper for the occasion, audience, and speaker. When speaking to an audience, it is very important to be aware that certain words can offend some people, even if they don't bother you. In fact, they may be words you are so used to hearing and saying that you don't even think about them as being potentially offensive.

Rule of Thumb: Never use any word that could possibly offend someone in the audience. Unless you know the word is OK with every person in your audience, do not use it.

There was a television show on HBO a few years ago called *Def Comedy Jam*, which featured young comedians. It was known for being especially raw language-wise, and performers regularly commented that they had to make their act more dirty to succeed on the stage there. However, in most situations you will encounter, the opposite is true. Discussing sexuality and body functions in a non-medical context or using swear words will only make your audience feel uncomfortable. It will prove you are unable to conduct yourself appropriately in professional situations.

Building Credibility By Using Appropriate Language:

- Avoid swearing.
- Avoid sexist language.
- Avoid racially insensitive language.

First, **avoid swearing** to build your personal credibility. A very interesting web site hosted by the Cuss Control Academy of Northbrook, IL, at cusscontrol.com, explains about what is wrong with swearing in professional situations. They argue, "Swearing imposes a personal penalty. It gives a bad impression, reduces respect people have for you, shows you don't have control, and is considered by many to be immature."

Also, **avoid sexist language.** When you make generalizations about women or men, you risk insulting your audience. While some sexist remarks are overt, like saying, "Women can't be presidents of companies," others are more subtle. For instance, always using "he" as a default pronoun, or assuming a nurse in a hypothetical example is a "she" may call attention away from your point and make the audience question your sensitivity to gender issues.

Naturally, we should **avoid racial insensitivity.** As Trent Lott discovered in the fall of 2002, even indirect racism can destroy your personal credibility. An example of subtle racism occurred in a speech last semester when a student said that in his neighborhood they believed in family values. There was a subtle assumption that other neighborhoods did not have these values. Another student referred to a group as "culturally deprived." All groups have culture. The culture of another group may not be the same as yours, but it is culture nevertheless. It will be impossible for you to have excellent rapport with your audience if you use language that is racially insensitive.

Conclusion

In this chapter we have discussed the importance of language in public speaking. Improving your language choices starts with improving your vocabulary. Clarity in language is essential and can be accomplished in six ways. Once the language is clear, it is fun to make it vivid. This is what makes the audience enjoy the speech. Finally, appropriateness is essential and includes avoiding swearing, sexist remarks, and racial insensitivity.

From Fright to MIGHT Moment

Vivid language will get your audience caught up in your speech. They will be so interested in your descriptions and word choices that judging you will be far from their minds.

Speakers' Secret

Oral language is different than written language.

- Oral language is less formal.
- Oral language uses shorter, simpler sentences.
- Oral language allows repetition.
- Oral language emphasizes the sounds of words.

Chapter 11: Terms & Concepts

Abstract words
Accurate language
Alliteration
Ambiguity
Antithesis
Clarity
Concise language
Concrete words
Connotative meanings
Denotative meanings
Familiar words
Figurative imagery
Jargon
Ladder of abstraction
Literal imagery
Metaphor
Multiple meanings
Parallelism
Personalize
Racial insensitivity
Repetition
Rhythm
Sexist remarks
Simile
Slang
Specific words
Vivid language

Work Cited

Schachtman, Tom. *The Inarticulate Society.* New York: The Free Press, 1995. page 11.

Activity #1: Understanding Chapter 11

Answer the following items as true or false.
Answers appear in Appendix C.

1. The language used in speech and in essay writing is very similar.	T	F
2. Denotative meanings of words are the dictionary-type meanings.	T	F
3. "Ship" is more concrete than "cruise ship."	T	F
4. Vivid language includes the use of imagery.	T	F
5. In most cases, the phrase "many people" is preferable to "many of us."	T	F

ACTIVITY#2: Slang and Jargon

Create a glossary of 3 slang and 5 jargon words you know, including the term itself, a sample usage, and a definition.

Example: **Stat**. "Get that gurney in here *stat*." A medical term meaning immediately. (Jargon)

Slang Words

1.

2.

3.

Jargon Words

1.

2.

3.

ACTIVITY #3: Connotative and denotative meanings

Circle the words below you perceive to be positive. *Draw a line through* the words you perceive to be negative. Work quickly and don't leave out any words:

Family	**Money**	**Broccoli**	**Freeway**
Marijuana	**Brown**	**Red**	**Age**
Fast	**Organized**	**Skinny**	**Children**

When you have finished, compare your responses to the words with 2-3 classmates. Why were some of your responses different?

Visual Aids

Now, what we got here is a little game of show and tell. You don't wanna show me nothing but you're telling me everything.- True Romance

They say a picture is worth a thousand words. How long would it take you to speak a thousand words?

Sometimes there are just things that words alone cannot express as well as a visual representation can. Picture the pain of a hungry child, the incredible rate of growth in a company, the complex structure of a cell, and the beauty of a wonderful selection of music.

What would you do if you were given the assignment to prepare and deliver a descriptive informative speech about your favorite painting. If your audience has never seen the painting, would you be able to communicate to them the image, color, light, contrast, texture, and emotion with just words and delivery? You might, and you should try, but you could also use a little help.

In the following chapter, we will explore why and how you might use visual aids to supplement speeches you may give.

Advantages of Visual Aids

Visual support can be as important as verbal support in making your ideas clear and interesting. The following are some advantages of using visual aids:

Visual aids clarify complex concepts. Many ideas can be made somewhat clearer by the use of visual aids. For some ideas, visual aids are absolutely necessary to achieve clarity. A student recently showed a visual aid of African elephants ten years ago and a second visual aid of African elephants today. The photographs showed the dramatic difference.

Visual aids convey difficult emotions. Visual aids can convey a powerful emotional message. Think, for example, of the Save the Children Foundation's advertisements. It is one thing for an audience to hear that a child is starving, but visualizing that child will have a more direct impact on the audience.

Visual aids show visual comparisons such as before and after. Maybe you are familiar with Slim Fast or Hair Club For Men commercials. Both ads show people before and after using the products to make their dramatic effects real to the audience.

Visual aids help improve recall. Audience members simply remember things better when they have not only heard them but also have seen them. Learning theory suggests that some people learn more easily when they can see a concept. Your visual aid will also enhance the entertainment value of your speech even for those who do not learn this way.

Visual aids add interest. It is sometimes hard to stay interested in words alone. The mind wanders. But it is hard not to pay attention to interesting visual aids on C-sections for dogs, the meaning of dreams, or how to take prize winning photographs.

Visual aids promote conciseness. Long, drawn out verbal explanations can be replaced by one well chosen visual aid. Several years ago a student showed an enlarged picture of a photograph she had taken of a hurricane in Kaui. The damage was immediately obvious.

Visual aids add to credibility. Well prepared visual aids will make you appear very professional. The opposite is true. Credibility is immediately lost when you show poorly prepared presentation aids with sloppy work, misspelled words, or grammar errors. Your hard work will pay off, but sloppy work will hurt you.

Visual aids support ideas. A visual aid can function as a form of proof for your ideas and demonstrate that an event happened or a relationship exists between two ideas. Consider how visual evidence, including crime scene photography and surveillance videos, is often used in courtrooms to prove a person's guilt or innocence.

Visual aids aid communication with new speakers of English. Audiences are more diverse than ever. Limited English audience members appreciate your visual aids as they help them understand your topic and points.

·Attention · persuavsiveness.

Types of Visual Aids

There are several things you can use that fall under the category we are calling "visual aids," and some aren't even visual.

VISUAL REPRESENTATIONS

The type of visual aid you are most familiar with is probably the **visual representation.** When you give a speech, you often cannot bring in the actual item you are discussing because of size, value, scarcity, or impossibility. For instance, if you wanted to let us know that 2 million Americans attend rodeo events, while only 1 million attend professional football games, you can't really bring in 3 million people to show to your classmates. You might create a two dimensional visual representation, such as a **graph** or **chart,** and mount it on a **presenting board.**

Graphs

A **line graph** consists of lines that are charted on a grid. A line graph is good for revealing trends by showing how information changes over time.

A **bar graph** contrasts two or more sets of data by means of rectangles of varying length. It is good for comparing quantities or magnitudes.

A **pie graph** shows a given whole that is divided into component wedges. A pie graph is excellent for showing proportions. The pie represents 100% and each slice of the pie is a percentage of the whole. · in relation to the whole

A **pictorial graph** shows comparisons in picture form.

Charts

A **flowchart** is a diagram that shows a step-by-step progression through a procedure or system.

An **information chart** is material arranged as a series of key points.

An **organizational chart** is a diagram that arranges relationships in a hierarchy.

A **table** arranges numbers or words systematically in rows and columns.

Drawings

Drawings include maps. Imagine a geography teacher lecturing without maps. Or, imagine election night coverage without showing which states are going for each presidential candidate.

Photographs

Photographs are realistic, unique and sometimes very dramatic. Only one person took the picture and the creativity, uniqueness, and appropriateness is hard to beat. Be sure photographs are large enough to be seen by the entire audience.

Computer Graphics

Much clip art is royalty free and can be used by students in their speeches. Other material can also be used. A picture of an artist, poet, or singer might add to your presentation. You can also make your own.

OBJECTS

Another type of visual you might use is an actual **object,** sometimes called a *prop.* If they are available to you, objects can make excellent visual aids. Showing the actual object leaves nothing for the audience to misinterpret.

Types of Visual Aids:

- Representations
- Objects
- Media

Occasionally, it works well to use yourself as the visual aid. One student wore his forest ranger uniform to give an informative speech on filtering water. Cultural speeches can be effective if you wear a costume from your culture. Be sure to get your instructor's approval as you will not be following the usual dress code for the formal public speech.

MEDIA

The growing importance of technology in our society has made media-based visual aids more popular. While technology has made including media such as video clips or computer animation easier, it has also increased the responsibility of the speaker to be fully prepared with a backup plan in case the equipment fails.

Audio Aids

Audio aids are presentational aids you can hear. A student in a public speaking class wrote an informative speech on the history of jazz. As part of it, she put together a CD of short jazz renditions representing each time period discussed in her speech.

Film Clips

A scene from a movie or film can sometimes prove a point better than any other way. In our highly visual society, audiences love films. Video clips should be very short. Unless you play a clip without sound and talk over it, you will not be speaking during this time. Video clips should add to your speech, not substitute for your words.

Overhead Transparencies

Overhead transparencies will be familiar to you as many instructors use them to enhance their lectures. You can make use of this traditional presentational aid. You could draw a picture, create a chart or graph, or even print text from your own computer. Make sure the font is large enough for all to see.

Computer Slideshows

Slideshow programs, such as PowerPoint, have become very popular presentation aids in the business world. However, many speakers choose to put their entire speech on computerized slides. If your audience can read your speech, why should they listen to you? Remember you are the more important than your visual aids, and don't let them overpower you.

No matter what type of visual aid you choose to use, you must prepare and use it correctly. There are several important ideas to keep in mind.

Preparing Your Visuals

Choose visual aids that enhance your speech. Your visual aid should serve a specific and identifiable purpose. A picture or graph just for the sake of having one does not enhance the speech. If you're not sure how your visual aid improves your speech, consider not using it.

Use visual aids sparingly. A mistake beginners and some professionals sometimes make is to have too many visual aids. We recommend between one and three visual aids for your classroom speeches.

Visual aids should contain one major idea. Concentrate on presenting one key point per visual. Limit the number of words to the absolute minimum necessary. If your audience is reading, they aren't listening to you. You can always add information verbally as you display the visual aid.

Keep the formatting of your visual aids consistent. Have a design plan for your aids. Use the same colors, fonts, upper and lower case letters, and styling.

Make sure visual aids are large. Every audience member should be able to see every piece of information you present. Use bold, easy-to-read lettering and take out all irrelevant information. Use bold letters and make them larger than you think you need. As a rule, use at least an 18 point font. Test it by going to the speech classroom and putting it up in the front of the room. Stand in the back of the room. Can you see it easily? If not, redo it.

Make your visuals attractive. They should reflect time and thought spent in their preparation. Pay attention to the details, because you will have many eyes focusing on them during your speech.

Pay attention to color. Have a consistent color theme. Keep the number of colors to a minimum, usually three to four. Use neutral colors for backgrounds, and contrast the background from the picture or text (i.e., no white on white). Avoid shiny colors like gold that will reflect light, and overly bright colors that will be unpleasant for the audience.

Your visual aids should look professional. Unless you are an artist, avoid hand drawing and writing your visual aids. Double check your visual aids for accuracy. Nothing is more devastating to a speaker's credibility than the moment he or she reveals a visual that is scrawled in poor handwriting, filled with grammatical or spelling errors, colored in with crayon, or made with cheap materials. The quality of your visual aids is a direct reflection of how much you care about your speech and your audience.

Make sure your visual aids are sturdy. Never use plain paper. It is too thin and flimsy. The strongest boards – matte board and foam core – are available at any art supply store. These boards will be easier to manage and are less likely to fall off an easel.

Explain statistics on your visual aids. Always clarify and simplify overly complex numbers, symbols, and terms. Round off statistics whenever possible. Charts and graphs are great ways to make numbers visually digestible. Statistics can be communicated more efficiently and effectively through graphs and charts than through long drawn out verbal explanations. Remember, more numbers does not mean a better visual aid.

Use graphics instead of words whenever possible. It can be difficult for audience members to read large amounts of text while also listening to you speak.

Avoid some common design mistakes, such as the following:

1. **Too many words**
2. **Too tight spacing**
3. **Too many fonts and colors**
4. **Too cluttered & crowded**

Practice and Rehearse With Your Visual Aids

Visual aids can be frustrating if you haven't become comfortable with them. Presentation boards can fall down. Lights in overhead projectors can burn out. Film clips can break. Every precaution should be made to avoid as many of these pitfalls as possible.

1. **Plan your method of presentation and display carefully.**
2. **Practice with any unfamiliar equipment, and have back-up plans in case something goes wrong.**
3. **Pre-test any and all mechanical systems before you speak.**

During Your Speech

After you have selected the type of visual aid to use for your speech, and have prepared it, your final concern is how you will use it within your speech itself.

Here are several guidelines to follow. Your instructor will probably show you even more handy tips.

- **Place the visual aids so that every person can see them.**
- **Control when the audience sees your visual aids.** Use a blank presenting board or other cover-up. Re-conceal your visual aids when you are done with them.
- **Stand beside your visual aid, never in front of or behind it.**
- **Talk to your audience not your visual aid. Maintain eye contact with the audience.**
- **Stand so your dominant arm is closer to the visual and you will not have to cross your body with your arm.**
- **Do not dim the lights during your speech.** Your audience will be more easily distracted and likely to sleep.
- **Do not use the blackboard/dry erase board.** Do not create your visual aids during your speech. It looks more professional to have them prepared in advance.
- **Explain the purpose of your visual to the audience.**

- **Avoid passing something around.** Speakers sometimes choose an item too small to pass the back row test. They try to solve this problem by circulating the item. This can be disastrous as it pulls attention from you to the item and invites the audience to talk to one another during your presentation.
- **Reveal one item at a time.** If you have a list of items, do not show them all at once. Show one item at a time. You can achieve this by covering remaining items with Velcro on a presentation board or with opaque strips on an overhead transparency.

Conclusion

Visual aids represent an excellent opportunity to impress and educate your audience. We have covered the advantages of using visual aids as well as some basic types of presentational enhancement. Most importantly, you now have important tips at your disposal for creating your visual aids and managing them during your presentation. If you follow this advice regarding visual aids, your speech will be not only a treat for the ears, but also a feast for the eyes.

FROM FRIGHT TO MIGHT MOMENT

Professional looking visual aids show the audience you are concerned about them and will help them form a positive impression of you. In addition, visual aids give you a breather, because people are focusing their attention on something other than you.

Speakers' Secret

Internet downloads and color photocopying have taken speech class visuals to a new level. It is now possible to create amazing looking visuals at a relatively low cost.

You can obtain pictures directly from websites by right clicking on the picture and choosing "Save Picture As…" Photocopy centers can enlarge a picture and print directly from the disk.

Chapter 12: Terms & Concepts

Audio aids
Computer graphics
Drawings
Graphs
Line graph
Media-based
Object
Overhead projector
Photographs
Presenting board
Prop
Table
Using a visual aid
Video clip
Visual aids
Visual representation

Activity #1: Understanding Chapter 12

Answer the following items as true or false.
Answers appear in Appendix C.

1.	Visual support can be as important as verbal support in making your ideas clear and interesting.	T	F
2.	Visual aids help improve recall..	T	F
3.	A pie graph is a visual that contrasts two or more sets of data.	T	F
4.	Information Charts are visuals that arrange relationships in a hierarchy	T	F
5.	While technology has made including media based visual aids more popular, it has also increased the responsibility of the speaker to be fully prepared with a backup plan in case the equipment fails.	T	F

ACTIVITY #2: Critique a Visual Aid

Your instructor will give you (or a group of you) a sample visual aid from a previous public speaking class. Even though you don't know for sure how it was used during the previous speech, critique the quality of the visual aid using the criteria explained in Chapter 14. Use this analysis to develop a one-minute presentation in which you evaluate the visual aid. **Be sure to use good technique for handling the visual aid during your presentation!**

Answer these questions about the visual aid:	YES	NO	Not Applicable
Does it have only one major idea?			
Is it consistent?			
Is it large enough for every audience member to see every piece of information on it?			
Is the text legible?			
Is the visual attractive?			
Is there a consistent color scheme?			
Does it look professional?			
Is it made form strong and sturdy materials?			
Is it creative?			
Is there too much text?			
Is it too cluttered or crowded?			

Chapter 13

Delivery

Your work is ingenious. It's quality work. And there are simply too many notes, that's all. Just cut a few and it will be perfect. -Emperor Joseph II, Amadeus

While the topic and content of a speech are certainly important, the manner in which you deliver your speech can drastically alter your audience impact. Do you remember from Chapter 1 that **interference** is an element in the communication process? Well, a speaker's delivery skills can help reduce vocal and nonverbal interference during his or her presentation. Additionally, advanced delivery skills can help a speaker to be more entertaining and emotional. They can also emphasize key concepts and ideas. This will further improve the overall experience for the audience.

How to Choose a Delivery Style

What delivery style did you use for your first speech in this class?

The first delivery issue you should consider when preparing your speech is the style. There are four styles: manuscript, memorized, impromptu, and extemporaneous. The more styles you have in your repertoire, the better you will be able to adapt your delivery to fit the occasion.

MANUSCRIPT

word to word

The first method involves speaking from a **manuscript**. When delivering a speech from a manuscript, the speaker writes out every word of the speech in advance and then reads from the script during the performance. The expectation is very high that the content will be strong since the speaker has had a chance to sculpt every single word.

When delivering a speech with a manuscript, it is essential that you still perform the speech, not just read it out loud. The tone of your voice must be conversational and energized, and you must make eye contact with the audience. As we will discuss later in this chapter, eye contact does not mean flashing your eyes in the direction of the audience a few times each minute. Manuscript speeches should be rehearsed many times so you are very familiar with the speech and have even memorized some important sections, like the beginning and the end.

Also, you must take care that your manuscript itself is easy-to-use and professional looking. Most speakers never get to use the fancy, transparent teleprompters that politicians and celebrities use. You will likely be holding your script in your hands, which can limit your ability to gesture. You may be standing behind a lectern, which conceals part of your body and creates a nonverbal barrier between you and your audience.

Four Ways to Deliver a Speech:

- Manuscript
- Memorized
- Impromptu
- Extemporaneous

Manuscript speeches are good to use in situations where every word counts, when what you're saying is complicated, or in situations when your emotions could get the best of you. When delivering a eulogy, for instance, you might need a script to keep you focused.

MEMORIZED

The second style of speech delivery is **memorized**. When you perform a memorized speech, you write it out word-for-word and deliver it with no notes.

It is very time consuming to memorize a speech, and even a well-memorized speech can be hard to recall when you are under the stress of performing. Sometimes speakers who memorize their content deliver it in a very flat tone with a blank expression. These speakers may find that because they are concentrating on what word to say next, they lose their connection with the audience.

Memorized speeches can be very effective when speakers know their material well enough to deliver it convincingly and connect with the audience. It can be very exhilarating when you speak with the confidence of knowing what you will say next and the freedom of delivering the speech without notes. You can focus on your listeners, see their facial expressions, and respond to their reactions.

For most situations in your life you probably won't have the time to memorize an entire speech. However, if you plan to deliver a speech multiple times it may be worthwhile to memorize it so you can refine your delivery.

IMPROMPTU

ice breaker

The third way to deliver a speech is **impromptu**. Impromptu speaking is when the speaker has limited preparation time. The speaker prepares an outline of the speech during the brief preparation time, if any is given at all. Then, he or she develops the subpoints and creates the wording while speaking.

Competition speech, known as "Forensics," allows students to compete in Impromptu Speaking. Students are typically given a quotation and are asked to speak for approximately 5 minutes after *just two minutes of preparation*. While it is challenging at first, speakers who practice improve quickly. Most competitors deliver thoughtful, interesting, and organized speeches.

Impromptu speaking is the most frequently used speaking style in our everyday lives. You will use these skills to answer tough questions asked by job interviewers or clients. You will also use Impromptu when making unexpected presentations during professional or community meetings.

Impromptu speaking, when done well, can be very impressive. As you know from experience, when a person is able to "come up with" something good in an impromptu situation, it is very impressive to others. This is partially why improvisational comedy (like the Groundlings) is so popular. They are also funny, which doesn't hurt.

Even though it is spontaneous, it is possible to prepare. Techniques for successful impromptu speaking are further addressed in Chapter 17.

EXTEMPORANEOUS

keyword outline

The last method of speech delivery is called **extemporaneous.** In this type of delivery, you prepare the complete content of your speech, including a very thorough outline, but do not write the speech out word for word. The speaker rehearses the speech several times and becomes extremely familiar with the material, then delivers the speech for an audience with the use of notes.

This style of delivery has many advantages. For one, the speaker tends to sound very natural and conversational because he or she is developing words and phrases naturally. The content can be altered based on audience analysis during the speech. If the audience seems bored with one section, you can proceed to your next main point. If they seem interested in a particular area, you can elaborate.

After you become skilled at researching and organizing your speeches, you will find preparing an outstanding speech using the extemporaneous delivery method can be done quickly and professionally.

In the extemporaneous speaking event at forensics competitions, students are given a current events topic and 30 minutes to prepare a structured 7-minute speech, including multiple source citations. Often, students finish preparing their outlines in just 10-15 minutes and use the rest of the time to rehearse their delivery!

If you are interested in becoming a teacher, you will probably become very familiar with this delivery style. If you think a 6-8 minute informative speech is difficult to perform with just a few notes, notice that your instructors can lecture for an entire class period with just a page or two of notes!

For this course, your instructor will likely assign a delivery style for each speech assignment. After you leave class, you will have to make that decision on your own. Be sure to weigh the advantages and disadvantages of each delivery style.

How to Use Your Voice

If your speech could be compared to a symphony, then your voice would be the instrument which plays the written notes. It is a highly flexible instrument and is capable of a wide range of vocal variety. It is also a delicate instrument, requiring careful use.

VOCAL TECHNIQUES

Projection

For beginning speakers, the most essential vocal technique is **projection.** It is essential for communication to occur that every audience member be able to hear every single word of your speech. This is achieved with vocal **projection,** sending your voice to different areas of the room. With a microphone and amplifier, projection is easily achieved. In many speaking situations, however, you won't have any support for your voice other than your own lungs and vocal cords. Projecting your voice requires good control of your breath and the use of your diaphragm muscle.

Volume Variety

Another vocal characteristic related to projection is **volume variety.** Variety in volume assists the audience in maintaining interest and involvement in what is being said, and helps to emphasize key concepts. In his famous speech, "I Have a Dream," Reverend Martin Luther King, Jr. used volume to accent and compliment his message. Lowering his voice to almost a whisper or raising it to a high crescendo has kept audiences past and present mesmerized by the delivery of his message. When students watch this speech, they sometimes will physically move their bodies closer to the television screen when he speaks softly, demonstrating how involved they are with him as a speaker. At the moments when he is loud and demonstrative, audience members can be seen sitting at attention ready to respond to his message. Though many speakers increase their volume for emphasis, few take advantage of the power of quiet moments. If you attempt this technique, remember you still need to project your voice out to everyone in the audience, even if your overall tone is quiet or hushed.

Vocal Techniques:

- Projection
- Volume Variety
- Pitch Variety
- Rate Variety
- Pausing
- Articulation
- Pronunciation

Pitch

Pitch is the placement of your voice on a musical scale, and **pitch variety** refers to a speaker's use of a range of high and low notes while speaking. In the same way we tend to like melodies in music that move up and down the musical scale, we also like to listen to speakers whose voices employ pitch variety.

Using a somewhat lower pitch than your typical speaking voice can help to emphasize a serious point, demonstrate anger, or add richness to descriptive language. It also adds **closure** to a sentence or an idea. If you have a chance to review any of your speeches on tape, listen to hear how frequently you let your voice drop in pitch. You may notice your voice dropping at the end of every sentence, or even in the middle of sentences. This can make your speech hard to listen to, because ideas are not linked – they are constantly being "closed." Of course, one of the most obvious places to use a drop in pitch to create closure is the last phrase of your speech.

Using higher notes during your speech can demonstrate excitement, positive emotional feelings, and add a sense of energy to your speech. Be careful, though, speaking at too high of a pitch or sustaining a high pitch for too long can be an irritation to your audience.

The opposite of a voice with pitch variety is a **monotone voice.** A monotone speaker uses very little pitch variety. This type of speaking is usually very low energy, doesn't emphasize the most important ideas in the speech, and doesn't hold the audience's attention very well. A famous example of a monotone speaker is the economics teacher from the film *Ferris Bueller's Day Off.* He asks questions to the class and then tries to elicit a response by droning, "Anyone? Anyone?" No one responds.

Rate

Rate is the cadence or speed of word delivery in your speech. At a minimum, it is essential that you speak at a reasonable rate for audience comprehension.

There are some unfortunate stereotypes connected with the rate at which people speak. A slow talking person who hesitates a lot is sometimes perceived as less intelligent. At the same time, speaking slowly can be very effective when delivering emotional messages or explaining difficult or technical concepts. It can even make you seem more confident. Speaking at a fast pace can be effective when you are trying to motivate an audience, because the energy can be exciting. However, speakers who constantly speak at a fast rate can seem nervous or even untrustworthy.

In general, the best speakers will have **rate variety** within each presentation. Changing your rate helps hold the interest of the audience, while giving them time to catch up and reflect upon your most important ideas.

Pausing

Pausing is the use of silence in your speech. Because it can be uncomfortable to be silent while standing in front of an audience, pausing may be the single most underused vocal technique. Not only does pausing allow the audience to catch up and react to what has been said, it also creates interest and allows for powerful nonverbal messages to be shared more clearly. Do not be afraid of silence. In our fast paced modern society, people expect there to be noise all the time. The uniqueness of silence allows you the power to bring their attention back to you and your message.

The opposite of a silent pause is the vocalized pause, in which we use **non-words** to avoid silence. Non-words were discussed in detail in Chapter 3.

Pronunciation

Pronunciation is the culturally agreed upon sounding of words. There is an expectation that people will pronounce words correctly, and the more education one has the greater this expectancy. For example, when interviewing for scholarships or jobs, one mispronounced word can be the difference between being declared the recipient or losing out. This applies equally to public speaking. When the audience realizes you have mispronounced a word, including a person's name, they may lose respect for you and begin to doubt the accuracy of others things you are saying. It is your responsibility as a speaker to know how to confidently pronounce all the words and names you use in your speech without hesitation.

Articulation

- the clarity of sound

Articulation is the clarity with which word sounds are uttered. The opposite of articulation includes slurring or mumbling words. Articulation allows you to be clear and understood so there is no miscommunication. Clarity connotes strength. Slurred speech connotes weakness or disinterest.

Many speakers do not realize they are articulating poorly, because everyday speech allows for a lot of latitude in articulation. We hear a friend ask us "Wajawaneet?" And we know that they mean, "What do you want to eat?" When we speak in front of an audience, they are probably not as familiar with our voice and speaking style, and would not understand that same phrase.

Being articulate may require you to overemphasize the movement of your mouth, lips, or tongue. You should also pay attention to how clearly you separate each word while you speak and avoid letting words run into one another. As a rule of thumb, we suggest that public speakers articulate at least 10% more clearly than they do in normal conversation.

VOCAL HEALTH

One of the worst things that can happen to a speaker is losing his or her voice. Illness is obviously a potential cause of a scratchy or lost voice, but other factors can also damage your voice – sometimes permanently. **Smoking** is a very common reason for vocal problems, particularly because of the importance of strong, deep breaths to project your voice. Over time, smokers' voices often become scratchy and coarse. Also, **overuse** of your voice can lead to a damaged voice. Shouting or talking for an extended period of time can cause hoarseness because of the wear and tear on your vocal cords. The effect of this damage is increased for speakers who do not support their voices properly using their diaphragm muscle, instead trying to create volume by tightening their vocal cords. The use of blood-thinning agents, like **aspirin**, as well as **alcohol** and **exposure to cold temperatures** can compound strain on vocal cords.

Over time, a lack of attention to your vocal health can lead to permanent vocal damage, including the development of small nodes on the vocal cords that may be irreversible. Popular performer John Leguizamo strained his voice so badly while portraying dozens of characters in his Broadway show that his doctor told him not to speak at all between performances. He had to write to people on a note pad all day to avoid irreversible damage to his voice from such intense use.

If you have a sore or scratchy throat, try to keep it warm and drink warm liquids to soothe it, such as tea with lemon. If your throat itches, instead of coughing, try to swallow. Avoid using products that numb the soreness in your throat. If you can't feel the pain and start talking, you might further damage your throat and pay for it later. In general, make sure you drink plenty of liquids to keep your throat and mouth from drying out, and get plenty of rest before giving a speech.

If you are really serious about improving the overall health and strength of your voice, consider taking an introductory voice and diction or vocal music class. These courses typically teach proper breathing techniques and will present exercises to help develop the quality and range of your voice.

How to Use Your Body

When you are in front of an audience, your body position, movement, and expression are an integral part of your performance. For some speakers, using your body effectively during a speech is a tremendous challenge. Often, speech anxiety manifests itself in the form of shaking hands, wiggly toes, funny facial expressions, and averted eyes. With some practice, however, it can be relatively easy to improve this aspect of performance. As you work on the techniques described below, be sure to use a partner, friendly audience member, or a videotape of yourself so you can have accurate feedback about your progress.

PHYSICAL TECHNIQUES

Posture

Posture is the physical placement of the body in the speaking situation. It is important because it conveys a sense of strength or weakness. Before you even utter words, the audience observes your body language. The physical manner in which you carry yourself reveals your perception of yourself. **Good posture** involves a straight back, shoulders rolled backwards, head held up straight and weight balanced evenly on top of a centered torso. This type of stance sends a message to the audience that you are confident, poised, and prepared. Bad posture in which the speaker is slouched or leaning sends a number of negative nonverbal messages, including a lack of confidence, a lack of poise, and a lack of credibility.

Controlled Movement

There are two types of body movement during a speech: unintentional and controlled. Unintentional movement includes fidgeting, clasping or wringing of hands, swaying, and pacing. These movements are somewhat acceptable in everyday conversation, but are magnified when you stand in front of an audience, creating a distraction from your message. They can also make you appear nervous, weak, or unprofessional. Instead, speakers should work toward **controlled movement**. Controlled movements can include transitional walking and gestures.

Physical Techniques:

- Good Posture
- Controlled Movement
- Facial Expressions
- Eye Contact

Transitional walking occurs when a speaker takes steps to nonverbally signal a change in the tone or topic of the speech, such as the transitions between main points. Always walk in the same way you would naturally take steps, but keep in mind these tips:

1. **Walk parallel to the audience; avoid backing away from them or walking toward them, unless it is for strong dramatic effect**

2. **Always talk and walk at the same time**

3. **Look at someone in the direction you are walking**

4. **Start with the leg that is in the direction you are headed**

5. **When you reach your new destination, reorient your whole body so you are still facing the entire audience. Never speak to just a portion of your audience.**

6. **When you are done walking, stop. Don't wander.**

7. **Never move while you are making a key point. Your nonverbal message ("transition to new idea") will contradict your verbal message.**

If you are disabled or injured and are unable to walk transitionally, consider making comparable transitional movements, if possible. This should be done if your speech is longer than just a few minutes. In general, though, the movement should not become a major distraction to the content of your speech. If mobility is challenging for you, stay in one place for your performance and focus on your vocal delivery and facial expressiveness to add interest and create a sense of transition.

Gestures

Gestures are controlled hand movements. They are important because they add expression, emphasis, and clarity. Natural gestures are fluid and have a definite beginning and ending. They are not choppy or artificial. Placement of gestures is important. Gestures are usually delivered above the waist. Gesturing too low is distracting. In contrast, random hand movements can distract the audience and make you appear nervous. Avoid too much repetition of the same gesture because it makes your speech seem over-rehearsed and unnatural. Avoid touching your hands together, playing with your note card, or holding a pen.

If you are not comfortable making gestures yet, just relax your arms at your sides while you speak. This may seem awkward, but looks very natural to the audience and helps them focus attention on your face and eyes. Avoid holding an arm bent at your waist, putting hands in pockets, hiding your hands behind your back, crossing your arms, or grabbing your arm with your hand.

Facial Expressions

Facial expressions are the movement of various parts of the speaker's face. Be aware that your face reveals many inner thoughts and feelings. Therefore, try to feel confident and your face will show it. Match your expressions to the tone of the speech. Eyebrows, lips, eyes, and even your nose can all add interesting accents to your words as you speak. At a minimum, your face should reflect your interest in your topic. It's surprising how many speakers appear to be bored by their own speeches!

Remember from Chapter 3 the importance of a speaker's **smile**. A smile radiates warmth and is calming to the audience. They are better able to establish a connection with you as a speaker because you appear friendly. Even if you are speaking about a very serious or controversial subject, you can begin your presentation with a smile. Making friends with the audience is even more crucial in these instances.

It has been said that the eyes are the windows to the soul. The expression **eye contact** indicates that the major way you make a contact with the audience is by looking at them and having them look back at you. An over-reliance on notes prevents this relationship. Hair falling in your face, wearing sunglasses, or wearing a hat or cap prevents this relationship. It appears you are hiding.

Though it is not always the case in other world cultures, in the United States the overwhelming expectation is that speakers will make **sustained eye contact** with their audiences. Speakers who avoid eye contact may be considered more nervous and less credible than other speakers. In general, work to sustain eye contact with each member of your audience for a complete thought or idea. Once the thought is completed, find the next person and begin the next idea. It is very challenging to deliver an entire speech using sustained eye contact. However, sustained eye contact will be extremely effective for you if you are willing to spend time mastering this technique.

From FRIGHT to MIGHT Moment

The secret to outstanding delivery is to talk with, and not to your audience. If you think of the audience as your friends, there will be less to worry about!

Speakers' Secret

When you use note cards for a speech, keep in mind the following tips:

- Only write on one side of each card. The audience wants to *hear* your speech, not *read* it.
- Make a practice set of cards as well as a performance set so your cards look fresh and wrinkle-free when you deliver the speech.
- Whenever possible, limit yourself to two cards so they can't get out of order.
- Only use one hand to hold your cards. They aren't that heavy.
- Don't gesture with the hand holding the cards – it's distracting!
- NEVER write out your speech really tiny and pretend to give an extemporaneous speech when you are really giving a manuscript speech. You won't fool anybody.

Chapter 13: Terms & Concepts

Articulation
Controlled movement
Extemporaneous
Eye contact
Facial expression
Gestures
Inflection
Impromptu
Manuscript
Memorized
Monotone
Overuse
Pausing
Physical characteristics
Pitch
Pitch variety
Posture projection
Pronunciation
Rate variety
Transitional walking
Vocal health
Volume variety

ACTIVITY #1: Understanding Chapter 13

Answer the following items as true or false.
Answers appear in Appendix C.

1. You can use 1-2 note cards for a memorized speech.	**T**	**F**
2. The most common type of speech you will give in life is probably a manuscript speech.	**T**	**F**
3. Smoking can impact your vocal health.	**T**	**F**
4. Movement during your speech can add energy and interest.	**T**	**F**
5. Good speakers tend to speak at the same rate for their entire presentation.	**T**	**F**

ACTIVITY #2: The Advantages and Disadvantages of Speech Delivery Styles

Complete the following table below using information from this chapter and your own thoughts:

Delivery Style	Advantages	Disadvantages
Impromptu		
Extemporaneous		
Memorized		
Manuscript		

Chapter

14

Informative Speaking

There's a war out there, old friend. A world war. And it's not about who's got the most bullets. It's about who controls the information. What we see and hear, how we work, what we think... it's all about the information! – Cosmo, *Sneakers*

In our world of cellular phones, wireless internet, and 24 hour news networks, a steady stream of facts and data is literally at our fingertips. We live in the age of information—an age in which technology increasingly helps us exchange messages in new and creative ways, but technology can only do so much. Often, we are responsible for crafting our own informative messages. Sometimes, we must deliver them live.

When have you been a teacher and helped someone learn? Studies indicate that the best sign of our knowledge about a subject is our ability to teach it to someone else.

If you have ever given someone directions, told someone how to make a particular food dish, presented a report, or taught any type of lesson, then you have been an informative speaker. You no doubt realized the difficulty of being clear and understandable when delivering complicated messages to a general audience. You may have also realized that some messages (like those contained in infomercials) often go beyond merely informing and actually try to influence audiences. So, what precisely is informative speaking?

The Goal of Informative Speaking

Like its name suggests, the goal of informative speaking is to inform, enlighten, teach, or educate the audience. We often evaluate informative speeches by asking ourselves a simple question, "Did I learn something from this presentation?"

Consider how the goal of informing differs from the goal of persuading an audience. Persuasive speakers often wish to change or influence an audience. They may wish to challenge what a person thinks or alter the way in which he or she behaves. Informative speakers, on the other hand, are interested in simply passing along factual information. To clarify this concept, consider the topic area of air pollution. A persuasive speech on this topic might address the harmful effects of air pollution and then urge audiences to buy electric cars or carpool. Conversely, an informative speech might report on the amount of pollution in our air or how electric cars operate. Notice the goal in the second two examples is not to change or influence what the audience feels or the way they behave. Rather, the primary goal is to educate listeners.

Make sure educating the audience is truly the primary goal of your informative speech. Sometimes without realizing it, we construct persuasive arguments in supposedly informative messages. If, for example, you were discussing a controversial issue such as cloning and you primarily informed the audience of all of the potential dangers of the practice, your speech would become an argument against cloning. Only if you also present the possible benefits of the research would you have a balanced informative speech.

A good example of a persuasive message hidden in an informative framework is the so-called "infomercial," commonly seen on late-night television. These 30 or 60 minute programs supposedly inform us about all the features of a great new product, but they do not really give us all the information, do they? Will they share the fact that their product is made of low-grade plastic? That it does not include a vital component (sold separately)? Or that it only works in certain climates? Be a little skeptical when listening to informative presentations. And remember, your audience may also be listening skeptically when you speak.

Types of Informative Speeches

Generally speaking, there are four types of speeches each of which shares the same general goal: to inform.

1. **A Speech of Description** educates the audience about something or someone through vivid and detailed descriptions ("The Splendor of Maui").

2. **A Speech of Demonstration** teaches the audience how to do something often through a step-by-step procedure ("How to Decorate a Wedding Cake").

3. **A Speech of Explanation** helps the audience understand how something works mechanically or systemically ("Why Earthquakes Occur").

4. **A Speech of Revelation** uncovers new information about concepts or objects like discoveries, theories, and inventions ("The Latest Breakthrough in Spinal Paralysis Research").

These categories are not completely distinct from one another. Your speech may belong to just one or maybe all of these categories. Regardless of the type of speech you present, make sure to keep in mind the following guidelines so your speech will be as engaging as it is educational.

The Three Golden Rules of Informative Speaking

RULE #1: DON'T BE BORING!

It's sad to say, but sometimes people are boring when presenting educational messages. Remember all those scholastic filmstrips and videos that put us to sleep in grade school? To avoid that horrible fate, first choose the right topic for your speech. Always be more concerned about what your audience already knows than what you already know. You cannot be *informative* if an audience already knows the information you are presenting. You will be *boring*. When choosing an informative topic, consider these two concepts:

"Need to Know"

Do your audience members *need to know* the information you will be presenting? In other words, is this topic socially significant? Great speakers present information that has a significant financial, medical, cultural, educational, or other important impact on the lives of their immediate audience.

"Neat to Know"

Besides being socially significant, information should also be interesting or *neat to know*. That is, the facts of your subject should immediately spark curiosity when you mention them.

Great informative topics, which fulfill both the *need* and *neat to know,* are sometimes hard to find. You will need to do a lot of thinking, talking with people, reading, and listening to find a true gem that is both important and fascinating. For a further challenge, try to find a topic that excites your public speaking instructor! After seeing hundreds of informative speeches a year, it will be difficult to find a topic that he or she has not yet heard, but it could happen.

Once you have sparked our curiosity through your dynamite topic, hold onto it by choosing vivid examples, telling exciting stories, and speaking with animated vocal delivery and facial expression. Show the audience just how exciting and interesting your information is by the level of interest you show towards your topic and by the enthusiasm you demonstrate in your own delivery style.

RULE # 2: BE THOROUGH!

When your primary goal is to educate, a careful and comprehensive discussion of your topic is vital. An informative speaker who leaves the audience with unanswered questions or unclear explanations has not been an effective teacher.

One reason why informative speakers fail to be thorough is that they try to teach too much and wind up not having enough time to cover everything. Make sure your topic is specific and your speech is focused so you can cover it completely. Teach a few things really well. Reinforce them with examples, visuals, and even activities. If you do this, your audience will not forget them.

Being thorough also means knowing your information inside and out. Since most of you are not experts in the subject you are discussing, a strong base of outside research will be necessary to construct this speech.

Thoroughness also requires that you clearly and simply explain all of the confusing words and complicated information you are presenting. You are speaking in front of a general audience who may not understand the jargon or processes involved in your topic. Through analogies, metaphors, definitions, and diagrams, we can often make complicated information easy to understand for most audiences.

RULE #3: GET ORGANIZED!

One of the first things beginning teachers learn is that effective instruction cannot happen without proper organization. Students grasp information better when it is presented in a structured format. Here are some common organizational frameworks for each type of informative speech. (These structures are described in greater detail in Chapter 8.)

A Speech of Description, especially when it concerns a place such as a city or a country, is often organized using a **spatial structure**. Take a look at a map and divide the area up into 2-4 main geographic regions. Each region can function as a main point in your final presentation.

A Speech of Demonstration is also called a "How-To" speech and often makes use of a **chronological**, step-by-step organizational pattern. Each step becomes a main point of the speech. If there are too many steps to make each one a main point, consider how you might group steps into phases. For example, if you were demonstrating how to make a type of food dish, you might first discuss the preparation phase, then the actual cooking phase, and finally, the serving phase.

A Speech of Explanation, which helps the audience to understand how something works mechanically or systemically, often uses the **structure-function sequence**. This is an organizational pattern in which your first main point describes the different components of your topic. The second and possibly third points explain the applications (or uses) of the subject.

The Three Golden Rules of Informative Speaking:

- Don't Be Boring
- Be Thorough
- Get Organized

A Speech of Revelation is often organized using a **topical pattern**. First, the speaker details the historical development of the new invention or discovery. Second, the speaker explains how it works. Finally, the speaker details the applications or benefits (as well as drawbacks) of this new discovery/invention.

Conclusion

In this chapter we have explained the function of informative speaking as well as a few guidelines. Remember that each of us has the capacity to become a teacher simply by preparing and delivering an effective informative speech.

From FRIGHT to MIGHT Moment

The fear of being boring is a concern for many speakers, but if your informative speech contains lots of personality, stories, and humor, you can be confident your audience will respond positively to your performance.

Speakers' Secret

Visual aids are very important in informative speaking, because many people learn new information better if they can see it as well as hear it.

For even greater effect, get your audience *involved*. Retention of material is almost twice as high if people do something as well as see or hear it.

Chapter 14: Terms & Concepts

Chronological Structure
Demonstration
Description
Explanation
Neat-to-know
Need-to-know
Relevance
Revelation
Spatial
Structure
Structure-Function Pattern

Activity #1: Understanding Chapter 14

Answer the following items as true or false.
Answers appear in Appendix C.

1. The primary goal of informative speaking is to educate the audience.	T	F
2. Only factual and accurate information should be used in informative speeches.	T	F
3. Generally speaking, there are four types of informative speeches.	T	F
4. Spatial structure uses a chronological, step-by-step organizational pattern.	T	F
5. Organization is one of the three golden rules of informative speaking.	T	F

Persuasive Speaking

You want free speech? Let's see you acknowledge a man whose words make your blood boil, who is standing center stage advocating at the top of his lungs that which you would spend a lifetime opposing at the top of yours. – President Shepherd, *An American President*

When was the Last time someone tried to persuade you?

Every day we are bombarded with messages that try to influence the way we think and behave. Gap commercials try to sell us that new pair of khakis. Public service announcements urge us to stay away from drugs. Politicians campaign to win our votes. Each of these scenarios is an example of a persuasive appeal. Soon, you will have to construct your own persuasive speech with its own specific appeal.

Although persuasion comes in many different forms, at the heart of each message is the desire to influence an audience. Influence is a broad term that can mean a dramatic change on the part of listeners or simply a subtle reinforcement of the way they already think or act.

Persuasive Goals

Persuasive speeches inherently seek to influence audiences in one or more ways.

1. **Belief-based Speeches** ask audiences to consider their fundamental beliefs about whether something is true or untrue ("Second hand smoke causes cancer.").

2. **Attitude-based Speeches** ask audiences to consider whether something is right or wrong ("Human cloning is immoral.").

3. **Behavior Based Speeches** ask audiences to consider their personal actions and whether a specific behavior should be stopped, adopted,

or changed ("We should put on our seatbelts every time we enter the car.").

4. **Policy Based Speeches** ask audiences to consider altering an existing policy (such as a rule or law) or to help create a new policy ("The California three-strikes law should be repealed.").

As you come across potential topics, ask yourself in which category a topic belongs. You may be able to neatly fit your topic in one category or you may discover it fits within two or more. For example, a speech on the topic of medical marijuana may seek to change listeners' beliefs ("There is no medical evidence to support marijuana's medicinal benefits") as well as behaviors and policies ("Vote against the legalization of medical marijuana.")

Persuasive Speeches Can Influence:

- Beliefs
- Attitudes
- Behaviors
- Policies

When discussing controversial topics like the legalization of marijuana, influencing an audience can be extremely difficult. This is especially true if audience members are firmly opposed to your position. Persuasion is easier said than done. But it's not impossible. In fact, several centuries ago, one of the most famous thinkers in Western philosophy had quite a bit to say about it.

Aristotle and Persuasion

One of the first people to formally discuss the idea of persuasion was the ancient Greek philosopher Aristotle. Aristotle was a student of Plato and tutor to Alexander the Great. Aristotle's many books include the *Poetics*, the *Metaphysics*, the *Politics*, and *Rhetoric* -- in which he delineates the three major aspects of persuasion: pathos, logos, and ethos.

PATHOS

In Aristotelian theory, pathos refers to the emotional appeal inherent in much of persuasion. When we become emotionally involved in a speaker's message, we are more likely to be influenced.

Think for a moment about recent ads and public service announcements dealing with cigarette smoking. Many use fear to get the message across. Remember the image of the woman smoking out of the hole in her neck? Sympathy is also a common appeal. When ads focus on the innocent victims of second-hand smoke, sadness is evoked to create influence. Other ads may employ humor. The image of the wilting cigarette, which is shown to support the idea that smoking causes impotence, is an example of this usage.

The idea is quite simple. Emotion creates engagement in an audience. This helps a speaker's ideas become more vivid and compelling. If we are engaged in a speaker's message, we are more likely to be influenced. As speakers, we can generate and employ many different types of emotional appeals including, but not limited to:

- **Fear**
- **Anger**
- **Sympathy**
- **Humor**
- **Patriotism**
- **Excitement**

So, how does a speaker generate these emotions in audience members? One method is to **use supporting materials** that have an emotional punch. Real-life stories about people experiencing hardship and/or joy may reach the hearts of listeners. Also, **using specific words that have an emotional quality** can generate pathos. Instead of saying, "Today my topic is dog bites," search for more emotional language like, "Today we'll uncover a horrible menace plaguing our playgrounds and neighborhoods: vicious dogs who attack innocent humans." Finally, **your delivery can create pathos**. Emotion is contagious. In your speaking style you should demonstrate the emotion you want audience members to feel. If audience members see the speaker becoming angry, sad, fearful, or excited, chances are good that they will start to feel the same emotions.

LOGOS

Emotion alone is not enough to ethically persuade an audience. Speakers must also use logos, or what we refer to today as logical appeal.

A logical speech is one that appeals to our sense of reason by using well-substantiated arguments. In simple terms, an argument is any claim that is supported by evidence. For example, in a student speech on auto mechanic fraud, the speaker made a claim in her introduction that this was a significant problem, worthy of her audience's attention. She supported this claim by providing not only emotional examples about real people who were victimized but also statistics from reliable sources about the number of people affected each year. Using numerical evidence as well as stories, she supported her claim and proved it was a significant topic.

As you can see from the preceding example, for an argument to make sense, it must not only use research and evidence, but also be constructed logically. Some forms of logical argument construction include:

Cause and effect: For example, "Since 90% of smokers experience some kind of health problem, we can logically assume that cigarettes cause serious health risks."

Inductive reasoning: These arguments begin with specific instance and move to a general claim. "Students, workers, and parents all report they experience unexpected drowsiness which harms their ability to perform simple tasks throughout the day. Obviously, sleep deprivation is a problem that affects many different types of people."

Deductive reasoning: These arguments start with a general claim and move to a specific conclusion. "Ours is a society based on the idea of individual freedom and non-discrimination. Thus, traffic officers who commit racial profiling by pulling over African Americans without cause are violating some of the foundations of American society."

These are just a few ways to construct arguments in your speech. There are many more. Your instructor may talk about others during class.

As a final note about logos, be sure to steer clear of any logical fallacies as you put together your arguments. Some logical fallacies include:

Bandwagon: "Everybody's buying Internet stocks; so should you!" Everyone is doing it.

Tradition: "We've never given plusses and minuses with letter grades at our college; we shouldn't start doing it now."

Hasty generalization: "Three students at our college experienced car robberies last semester. Campus crime is a huge problem here."

False dichotomy (offering only two choices when there are other options): "Either you support the right for all women to terminate their pregnancy or you are totally opposed to abortion in all instances."

ETHOS

Ethos is the final aspect of persuasion discussed by Aristotle. Ethos refers to the credibility of the speaker. Research indicates the more credible a person is perceived to be by an audience, the more persuasive power he or she will wield.

Advertisers use ethos all the time to sell products. Take, for example, basketball star Kobe Bryant and his involvement with Adidas shoes. Kobe's professional credentials combined with his likeable personality made him an extremely effective spokesperson. Unfortunately, most of us do not have the immediately recognizable ethos of Kobe. We must work harder to establish credibility during our speeches.

The first step is discovering the two general questions audience members ask themselves when determining a speaker's credibility:

Is the speaker an expert, or at least competent to speak on a subject?

Does the speaker possess an honest and likeable character?

The fact that Kobe is a great basketball player is not the only reason why he is such a credible spokesperson for Adidas. There are lots of great players. For many people, Bryant is also perceived as likeable, sincere, and trustworthy.

Once you realize that credibility is made up of a speaker's perceived expertise and character, you can begin to analyze how certain aspects of speechmaking affect our individual credibility.

Factors influencing our perceived expertise and character include:

The Three Tools of Persuasion According to Aristotle's *Rhetoric*:

Pathos: Emotional proof in which you use meaningful delivery and real-life examples to reach our hearts.

Logos: Logical proof in which you use research and clear arguments to appeal to our sense of reason.

Ethos: Personal proof in which you use your own character and competence to create an aura of credibility.

- **Personal experience**
- **Use of research and supporting materials**
- **Delivery and appearance**
- **Language choices**
- **Relationship you establish with the audience**

Ways to Organize Persuasive Speeches

Thus far, we have discussed persuasion from a theoretical standpoint. Let's move to some of the specifics of this speech by taking a look at three different ways to structure a persuasive speech.

METHOD ONE: *THREE REASONS*

The **Three Reasons** structure is the most simple of the patterns we will discuss. Just because it is simple, however, does not mean it is ineffective. In this type of speech, the speaker makes a claim and then supports that claim using three separate reasons. Consider the following rough outline:

Topic: Capital Punishment

Claim: Capital punishment is an ineffective means of punishing criminals in our society.

Reason One: Capital punishment does not deter crime.

Reason Two: Capital punishment costs more money than imprisonment.

Reason Three: Capital punishment is inherently racist.

Of course, this is a very brief outline. In a formal outline, each of these points would need to be supported with convincing subpoints and appropriate research. However, this example does demonstrate how each reason individually supports the overall claim. Together, these three reasons have the potential to create a convincing argument.

METHOD TWO: *PROBLEM/CAUSE/SOLUTION*

The **Problem/Cause/Solution** speech is an intermediate pattern for persuasive speeches which, like its name suggests, first convinces listeners that there is a problem worthy of their attention, then uncovers the factors that are responsible for the problem, and finally outlines specific steps that will fix the problem. Each step is a main point of your speech, and each is crucial to the overall appeal you are creating. Here's another rough outline to consider:

Topic: Hand washing

Claim: The lack of hand washing is a serious health hazard in the United States.

Main Point One (Problem): Many people do not wash their hands regularly, and this harms our society.

Main Point Two (Cause): People do not wash their hands because they think they are too busy, and because they do not know the potential health hazards.

Main Point Three (Solutions): If businesses, organizations, and individuals followed a few simple hand-washing guidelines, we could stop this health hazard.

Again, this is very brief and needs much more development. For a more detailed example of this structure, please refer to the sample speech in Appendix B.

You may think the Problem/Cause/Solution structure requires a lot of informational steps before getting to the persuasive part (solutions). However, sometimes persuasion involves giving a lot of information and allowing audience members to draw some of their own conclusions. The persuasion is subtle, not aggressive. You need to take time to develop the problem and its causes for the audience instead of just jumping up and telling them what they should do and believe.

METHOD THREE: *MONROE'S MOTIVATED SEQUENCE*

Let's now consider an advanced persuasive structure that builds upon many of the concepts introduced in the Problem/Cause/Solution format. Allan Monroe was a speech professor in the 1930's whose five step psychological approach to persuasion has certainly stood the test of time.

His approach is so influential, in fact, that it even bears his name: **Monroe's Motivated Sequence.**

Step One — Capture the Attention of the Audience

This should be painfully obvious by now. If listeners are not paying attention to a speaker, there is no way that speaker can create influence. Your introduction must make audiences *want* to listen to you.

Step Two — Create the Need for Change

Before audience members will change their beliefs, attitudes, or behaviors, a speaker should tell them why change is necessary in the first place. Persuasive speakers often describe the inadequacy of the present situation to accomplish this step. For example, if you were trying to persuade listeners to drink more water, you must first demonstrate that most people do not drink enough water, and that this lack of water in our diet creates a number of health hazards. In a Problem/Cause/Solution speech, the need step corresponds to both the problem and cause areas.

Step Three — Satisfy the Need

Now that the audience has been primed to see that change is necessary, they are ready for a specific plan that will fulfill these needs. The satisfaction step does just that. Often, the satisfaction step details several proposals that communities, institutions, and people can adopt that will satisfy the need and thus fix the problem. To continue with our example about drinking water, you might detail the ways in which schools, businesses, and peers could adopt specific policies that would encourage citizens to drink eight glasses of water every day. In a Problem/Cause/Solution speech, the satisfaction step is similar to the solution area.

Step Four — Visualize the Results

Audience members like to know that if they do what the speaker recommends, positive outcomes will ensue. In the visualization step, the speaker explains the benefits a listener will experience if they implement the plan outlined in the satisfaction step. In our speech about water consumption, you might describe how drinking eight glasses of water every day decreases our chance for cancer and heart disease, aids our bodies in digestion, and improves the overall quality of our skin.

Step Five — Call to Action

Finally, the audience is ready for your specific persuasive plea. The call to action should be personal and easily accomplished by everyone in your audience. The call to action in our water speech is clear: drink eight glasses of water every day, and encourage your friends and family members to do the same! In a Problem/Cause/Solution speech, the call to action will undoubtedly occur somewhere in your conclusion. Often, speakers use the call to action as the last line of their speech.

Monroe's Motivated Sequence is a more complex organizational structure than either the Three Reasons or Problem/Cause/Solution approach. As you decide the most appropriate structure for your speech, consider your topic as well as your persuasive goal. Topics that seek to influence beliefs or attitudes are often best suited to the first approach. If you want to directly influence listener actions and behaviors, you may want to use the Problem/Cause/Solution structure, or, if you're feeling brave, you may want to give the five steps of Monroe's Motivated Sequence a try.

Conclusion

In this chapter, we have taken a look at the theoretical foundations of persuasion as well as practical applications of this theory. On the next few pages you will find a detailed breakdown of the *Problem/Cause/Solution* structure (which can also serve as a worksheet for your own speech.) You will also find sample persuasive speeches in Appendix B.

From FRIGHT to MIGHT Moment

Persuasive speaking is all about influencing the audience. Instead of worrying about your own fear, focus on the various ways in which you might impact your audience. Speakers in the past who argued for civil liberties or against social injustice changed millions of lives. Aren't we glad they fought through their fear?

Speakers' Secret

Sometimes persuasive speakers go overboard and start yelling at their audience.

While it's good to care about your topic, most people don't respond to scolding. You can be influential while still being our friend. No matter how serious the subject matter, a smile and pleasant demeanor will make audiences more prone to accept your message.

Chapter 15: Terms & Concepts

Action
Appeal to tradition
Argument
Aristotle
Attention
Attitudes
Bandwagon
Behaviors
Cause and Effect
Claim
Deductive Reasoning
Ethos
Evidence
False dichotomy
Harms
Hasty Generalization
Inductive Reasoning
Logical Fallacy
Logos
Monroe's Motivated Sequence
Need
Pathos
Persuasion
Policies
Problem-Cause-Solution
Reasoning
Satisfaction
Scope
Testimony
Three Reasons
Values
Visualization

Works Cited

Monroe, Alan H. and Ehninger, Douglas. *Principles of Speech Communication, Sixth Brief Edition.* Scott Foresman: 1969.

Activity # 1: Understanding Chapter 15

Answer the following items as true or false.
The answers appear in Appendix C.

1. Classroom speeches are the only place we come into contact with persuasive appeals.	T	F
2. Ethos was the term Aristotle used to describe logical appeal.	T	F
3. You should avoid using emotion in a persuasive speech.	T	F
4. Inductive reasoning moves from general to specific.	T	F
5. In the problem-cause-solution format, the solution is the most important part of the speech.	T	F

☆

Informative	Persuasive
Teacher	Leader
Understanding (stress)	Emotion
Address Listeners as Individual	Address ~~lead~~ Listeners as a group.
~~Lit~~ Little Commitment	Great deal.

- All persuations are self-persuation.

5-7 mi

Activity #2: Problem/Cause/Solution Worksheet

General Goal:

Specific Purpose:

Introduction

I. Attention Device:

II. Topic Revelation Statement:

III. Significance Statement (Use a source.):

IV. Preview of Main Points:

Body

TRANSITION into first main point, an explanation of the problem:

I. First Main Point:

A. Definition of the Problem:

B. Scope of the Problem (Who is affected? Where?):

C. Harms of the Problem:

1. Economic (cost to society, individuals, etc.):
2. Environmental (conservation, safety, aesthetics, etc.):
3. Societal (justice, freedom, equality, sovereignty, etc.):
4. Psychological (pain and suffering, depression, rage, guilt, etc.):
5. Physiological (death, illness, injury, etc.):

TRANSITION into **second main point** (II), the causes of the problem:

II. Second Main Point

A. First Contributing Cause to the Problem:

B. Second Contributing Cause to the Problem:

TRANSITION into **third main point** (III), the solutions to the problem:

III. Third Main Point

A. Policy Changes Needed to Solve the Problem (if any):

B. Personal Action Changes Needed to solve the Problem (if any):

C. Attitude or Belief Changes to Solve the Problem (if any):

Conclusion

I. Statement to Review Topic and Main Points

II. Lasting Thought:

III. Final Call for Action:

Works Cited

Activity #3: Persuasive Topics

Come up with some possible topics for different types of persuasive speeches:

Desired Influence	Sample Topic	Your Topic Idea
Attitude-Changing or Reinforcing	Skateboarders have rights of way, too.	
Belief-Changing or Reinforcing	Capital punishment is wrong.	
Action-Changing or Reinforcing	Donate blood.	
Policy-Changing or Reinforcing	Let's maintain federal funding for the arts.	

Chapter

16

Speaking Outside the Classroom

Surveys show that the #1 fear of Americans is public speaking. #2 is death. Death is #2! That means that at a funeral, the average American would rather be in the casket than doing the eulogy! - Jerry Seinfeld

What is a famous political speech you remember seeing or hearing about?

What was the goal of that speech?

When many people think of public speaking, they imagine a famous politician or business executive standing at a lectern in front of a huge audience. They might imagine TV cameras recording the event as the speaker delivers a formal speech from a manuscript or a teleprompter. Situations such as these are certainly public speaking events, but they are just one in a long list of the occasions in which people speak to an audience. Each day, ordinary people deliver important speeches in commonplace situations for a variety of reasons. For example, you may have to perform a presentation for your job, give a toast at a best friend's wedding, deliver a eulogy, or even tell a story to a group of people at a party. Though you might not think of them as traditional speeches (and though they rarely entail the same exact type of specific organizational structures or research requirements as, say, an informative or persuasive speech) each of these communication events involves many of the same principles as a classroom speech.

In this chapter, we will first discuss speeches traditionally presented on special occasions, and, second, outline the everyday speeches many of us will find ourselves delivering.

Special Occasion Speeches

Most important events have a speaker. Graduations, weddings, and funerals are just a few examples. Because each special occasion is unique, the specific requirements and expectations for each speech will vary from situation to situation. However, special occasion speeches still have one of the three major goals of public speaking: to inform, persuade, or entertain.

SPECIAL OCCASION SPEECHES TO INFORM

Speech of Introduction

Most featured speakers are introduced to the audience before they speak. If you find yourself introducing another speaker, it is up to you to set the stage for a successful performance. The primary goal of this speech is to inform the audience about the speaker. Tips:

- **Research the speaker**. Consult his or her resume or arrange a short interview to ensure you have the most accurate information available. Focus on the speaker's achievements in your speech to build up his or her ethos. You may also want to find out something about the speech topic. Be sure to give the audience any information they need to fully understand the speaker's presentation.

- **Don't steal the spotlight**. Remember, audiences are not there to see you. Your speech should be short and focused exclusively on the speaker.

- **Speak extemporaneously**. If you need a set of brief notes, use them. But keep your delivery natural and conversational. Do not read from a manuscript.

Award Presentation

When an organization or institution honors someone with an award or gift, someone has to present the award. This speech, like the introductory speech, is designed to primarily inform. Tips:

- **Clarify the nature of the award**. What does it honor? Why is it given? Are there any past recipients you might mention?

- **Explain the recipient's qualifications and traits.** Be sure to praise the winner so that the audience understands why this person is so deserving of the award.

- **Make sure your speech is short and to the point.** Remember to stay focused on the recipient and the reason for the award presentation.

Award Acceptance

If you ever win the Nobel Prize, or are simply honored as employee as the month, you may be expected to give a speech of acceptance. Tips:

- **Be gracious**. Thank the presenter, acknowledge the organization that sponsors the award, and, if you feel it's appropriate, thank the people in your personal life that helped you reach the achievement. If other people were nominated, you may want to mention them, as well.

What award would you like to accept the most? What would you say during your acceptance speech?

- **Choose the right delivery style**. If you have been nominated or know beforehand you will win, you may want to prepare an extemporaneous speech. You do not want to appear too assured, however. Award winners who sound overly prepared can seem arrogant or self-obsessed. Audiences like speeches that are genuine and heartfelt.

- **Keep it short**. If you've ever watched the Academy Awards™, you know that long acceptance speeches can be boring. You may not have an orchestra that will cut you off if you speak too long, but you will see some glazed eyes if you are long-winded.

SPECIAL OCCASION SPEECHES TO PERSUADE

"Persuade" may seem like too strong a word to accurately describe the next two speeches. However, both are designed to influence, inspire, and move an audience. In that sense, they are persuasive.

Eulogy

This speech is delivered at a funeral to memorialize a person who has died and help audience members reconcile their emotions. Tips:

- **Write the speech on behalf of the whole audience, not just yourself.** Remember you are just one person who knew the deceased. Try to account for, or at least acknowledge, each of the different roles and relationships in this person's life. One way to begin to accomplish this is to interview other people so you might share memories from a variety of perspectives. As you think about the structure of a eulogy consider using a chronological pattern to help you account for the entirety of the deceased's life. Finally, if other people are speaking, you may want to coordinate your speeches so you don't overlap in your content.

- **Use a manuscript.** Remember, when emotion might get the better of you, a manuscript will help you maintain control and composure. If you are delivering a eulogy, no one will think less of you for using a script. Even with a word-for-word script in hand, you may experience a swell of emotion that could make speaking difficult. Crying or taking a moment to compose oneself during a eulogy is not a sign of weakness, nor is it considered dropping the ball. It is just a natural response to a difficult, emotional situation.

- **Be sure the eulogy is appropriate.** Appropriateness is crucial in emotional contexts like a funeral. Use of humor may be fine in one eulogy, and not another. Also, a funeral is not the right time to divulge secrets or awkward moments from a person's life. Being sensitive and appropriate means taking into account the circumstances of the person's death and the religious or spiritual dimensions of the funeral, and then using your common sense about the type of eulogy you will deliver.

Epideictic Speech

This speech is delivered to praise or condemn someone or something. Epideictic speeches are delivered in situations such as a retirement dinner in which you might, for example, praise a longtime co-worker or a political rally in which you might speak for or against a candidate for office. Even performances such as commencement speeches can be considered epideictic speeches since they are typically delivered to praise an institution and its graduating students. Tips:

- **Remember Aristotle.** Epideictic speeches are essentially persuasive speeches. As such, they must be grounded in ethos, pathos, and logos. Instead of simply expressing your opinions, take time to carefully research and structure your speech, and then deliver it using the tools discussed in this class.

- **Craft your language carefully.** The best epideictic speeches make strong use of vivid, clear, and appropriate language. You may also want to consult quotation books to find particularly inspirational words from other people.

SPECIAL OCCASION SPEECHES TO ENTERTAIN

Toast

A toast is a speech of thanks or well wishing given with drink in hand, often before dinner celebrations like weddings and anniversaries. Tips:

- **Make it personal or emotional.** When delivering a toast, focus on ways to use humor, excitement, or personal opinions to make the speech meaningful.

- **Use your audience.** Always refer to the people sitting at the table in your toast so everyone feels involved in the moment.

- **Keep it short.** People are hungry, after all.

After Dinner Speech

An After Dinner Speech is a funny, entertaining speech on a light topic often delivered after a luncheon or dinner. Tips:

- **Make sure your speech has a point.** Unless you are Chris Rock, a consistently funny speech is hard to craft. So don't try to be a comedian. Be yourself, give a speech that has a message, and throw in humor when it seems appropriate.

- **Pick the right topic.** This is true for any speech, but after-dinner speeches have some special requirements. Since this is an environment in which people are expecting to be entertained, make sure your topic is light and not offensive. Try to find a topic area that is new and creative and also has some significance to your audience.

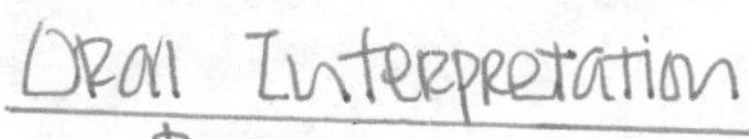

Everyday Speaking Occasions

There will be other speaking situations in your everyday life that may not be as momentous as the situations described on the last few pages, yet they are still important. Each of the following speeches will present different challenges, but skills you learn in this class can prepare you to handle each of the following confidently and effectively:

- **At school:** teach, deliver a lecture, tell a story

- **At place of worship:** preach, deliver a sermon, tell a story
- **At court:** argue your case, testify
- **At your business:** deliver sales presentations**,** interview
- **At the legislature:** debate, testify, hold a press conference
- **At the theater:** act

Conclusion

This chapter is intended to remind us that public speaking does not occur only in a speech class. On special (as well as not so special) occasions, we deliver real-world presentations to many types of audiences. Consider this class as a laboratory in which you experiment with different skills and concepts to prepare you for all the speeches you will encounter outside the classroom.

FROM FRIGHT TO MIGHT MOMENT

We fear the unknown.
Public speaking is an unknown experience for most people. You can lessen this fear by speaking as often as possible, not just in this class, but in real-world situations you encounter.

Remember that the speeches you prepare during this course won't necessarily resemble speeches you will be asked to give outside the classroom.

However, the skills and experience you gain from these classroom speeches can easily be applied to nearly every speaking situation you will encounter throughout your life.

Chapter 16: Terms & Concepts:

After Dinner speech
Award Acceptance speech
Award Presentation speech
Epideictic speech
Eulogy
Everyday speeches
Speech of Introduction
Toast

Activity #1: Understanding Chapter 16

Answer the following items as true or false.
Answers appear in Appendix C.

1. You will probably never have to give another speech after this class.	T	F
2. An Epideictic Speech is a speech about someone who has recently died.	T	F
3. Special occasion speeches are never persuasive.	T	F
4. When introducing someone, always do some research in advance.	T	F
5. Long award acceptance speeches are always enjoyable for audiences.	T	F

Activity #2: Brainstorming

Instead of just envisioning your future as a public speaker, let's time warp to the future and brainstorm a few lists about speeches you might one day give:

Possible presentations your desired profession might require:	Possible speaking occasions your personal life might require:	Possible speaking occasions your involvement in clubs, community groups, church or other groups might require:

See the "Time Warp Speech" assignment in Appendix A for a speaking assignment associated with this activity.

Impromptu Speaking

"I guess we all do unexpected things sometimes, don't we?" - Gleaming the Cube

Have you ever asked your parents for money? If so, chances are you gave them an impromptu speech.

We don't always have two weeks to prepare a speech. More often than you might believe you will be called upon to give a speech on the spur of the moment. These impromptu situations will require you to call upon much of what you have learned so far in this public speaking class, and it will ask you to add a few new techniques, as well.

Impromptu Speaking in the Real World

You are at a meeting and the person who is supposed to introduce the guest speaker is caught in traffic. The president of the organization asks you to do the honors.

You are at work and the business changes to a topic about which you feel passionately. Suddenly, you want to speak, be understood, and move people to your side of the issue.

You are interviewing for an important job and are asked a completely unexpected question. Faces from the interview panel stare at you, awaiting your answer.

In these situations, and many more, you will be thankful that you have training in impromptu speaking. Impromptu speeches occur when a speaker has little or no preparation time. The speaker must prepare a quick mental outline, and choose his or her exact wording for the speech as the speech is in progress. For many, this can be a very intimidating type of speaking, even though we do it every day.

Preparation: Your Mind is a Great Storehouse of Knowledge

Contrary to popular belief, you can prepare for impromptu speaking. In a sense, all of your life is preparation for it. Everything you know is part of the arsenal of ideas available to you for an impromptu speech. Sources include books you have read, theories you have learned in class and elsewhere, movies you have seen, biographies, novels, stories and articles you have read, and much, much more.

In order to prepare in advance of a speaking day for this unique type of speaking, it is helpful to write down many of the things you know. You will probably be surprised at the vast storehouse of information in your mental archive when you take the time to reflect. Unfortunately, unless we keep this information well organized, we won't have quick access to it in impromptu situations.

There are many ways to organize your knowledge. One approach is typically left brain, known as **making lists**. The other is more right brain, known as **mind mapping**. Search your brain for those fascinating tidbits of knowledge and create an organizational pattern to aid recall. Students who are more comfortable with lists may find activity #2 at the end of this chapter helpful. Students who are more comfortable with random retrieval of information may want to try activity #3. After you have organized your knowledge a bit, study your list or map before your classroom impromptu assignment is due.

You can also prepare for impromptu speeches by **anticipating possible topics you might be asked to discuss**. For instance, you might invest just a little time thinking in advance about the questions a job interviewer will ask you, or imagining possible clients you could encounter while at a conference. This little time you spend anticipating and preparing could have a big payoff when you have just the right answer or product pitch on the tip of your tongue.

Organizing Your Impromptu Speech

A common mistake impromptu speakers make is speaking without structure, and rambling on too long. A solution to both of these problems can be found by using a solid structure for each impromptu speech you deliver, making sure your speech has a beginning, middle (with main points), and an end, all before you even begin speaking. A very simple outline will work well for impromptu speaking. Instead of making it more difficult as you might think; it will make it easier to remember what you want to say if you have an outline.

Introduction:

1. **Attention Getter**
2. **Topic Revelation Statement**
3. **Preview**

Body

I. First Main Point

II. Second Main Point

III. Third Main Point

Conclusion

1. **Summary**
2. **Return to Attention Getter**

A sample speech using this structure can be found in Appendix B.

To assist you in selecting your main points, many of the organizational structures of speeches we discussed in Chapter 8 can be quickly applied to an impromptu speech.

Some simple impromptu main point structures you may wish to try include:

1. **Past, present, future**
2. **International, national, state, local**
3. **Philosophical, ethical, political, social**
4. **Costs, benefits**
5. **Pros, Cons**
6. **Biography, Accomplishments, Greatest Accomplishment**
7. **Example #1, Example #2, Example #3**

Delivering Impromptu Speeches

By their very nature, impromptu speaking situations are unpredictable, and therefore, can create stress and anxiety in a speaker. Somehow, though, many people are able to deliver impromptu speeches calmly and confidently without ever breaking a sweat. How do they do it? Well, many professionals will tell you they simply choose to **seem confident**, even if they don't feel confident. You can seem confident by maintaining eye contact, speaking slowly, controlling your body movement, and smiling.

Also, if you want to improve as an impromptu speaker, you need to work on your **fluency**, or the smoothness with which the right word comes out of your mouth at the right time. Practicing impromptu speeches is actually a great way to improve your overall fluency as a speaker, since it forces your mind to work more efficiently to select appropriate language.

Finally, it is important to **be succinct** when you are giving impromptu speeches. When you are out of ideas, review and conclude your speech. Since you haven't rehearsed your speech, you may not have a good sense of how much time has passed since you began. If you hear yourself repeating an idea you already shared, it's probably time to wrap it up.

Mental Preparation Before the Speech

Try this thought process:

1. **Choose a topic (unless one was given to you) and formulate a position on that topic.**
2. **Choose your organizational structure.**
3. **Review your storehouse of knowledge for some concrete examples, facts, and reasoning to support each main point.**
4. **Develop an attention device so it can be used at the beginning of the speech as well as part of the conclusion.**
5. **Mentally review parts 1-4, then deliver the speech.**

CONCLUSION

Keep in mind that giving great impromptu speeches is not unlike running a mile. If you have never done it before, the first try may seem impossible, but if you keep it up you are soon flying around the track.

FROM FRIGHT TO MIGHT MOMENT

The more knowledge you accumulate, the easier it will be to come up with examples that develop your ideas. There is less to fear when you have knowledge about how to construct a speech in its simplest form. Every day when we speak to friends and co-workers, we give many impromptu speeches using knowledge we have gained.

Practice what you speak!

Speakers' Secret

You know more than you think you know! Do a little archaeology on your own brain and try to dig up facts and stories you learned years ago, then use this information in an impromptu speech. If you use what you know, you will remember it even better next time around.

Chapter 17: Terms and Concepts

Fluency
Impromptu
Succinct

ACTIVITY #1 : Understanding Chapter 17

Answer the following as true or false.
Answers appear in Appendix C.

1. No preparation is possible for impromptu speaking.	**T**	**F**
2. Impromptu speaking is less important than all the other types of speaking.	**T**	**F**
3. People are asked to give impromptu speeches during their work day.	**T**	**F**
4. Impromptu speeches occur when a speaker has little or no preparation time.	**T**	**F**
5. There is only one organizational pattern for impromptu.	**T**	**F**

ACTIVITY #2: Listing What I Know

Instructions: Write an example of each of the following categories you would feel comfortable discussing before your classmates.

Example: Favorite movie --- Spider-Man

1. Favorite movie star
2. Favorite character in a movie
3. Favorite television show comedy
4. Favorite television show drama
5. Favorite news show
6. Favorite news anchor
7. Favorite rock star
8. Favorite older musician
9. Favorite song
10. Favorite piece of music video
11. Favorite classic book
12. Favorite modern fiction book
13. Favorite modern nonfiction book
14. Favorite fairy tale
15. Favorite fairy tale character
16. Favorite cartoon character
17. A theory from psychology
18. A theory from political science
19. A theory from history
20. Noteworthy politician/statesperson
21. Most interesting criminal trial

ACTIVITY #3: Mind Mapping What I Know

Directions: Start by drawing a circle on this page. Within the first circle, list an example of something you know that could be used in impromptu speaking. Every time you think of a new idea place it within a new circle. Draw lines to link related ideas. It won't take you long to fill this page with circles and ideas.

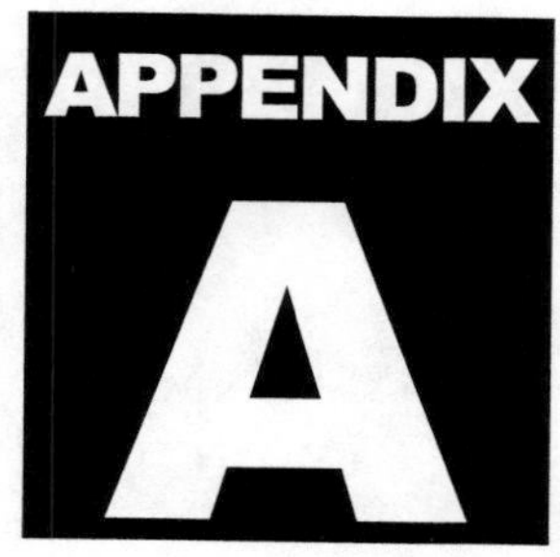

Speech Assignments

Icebreaker Speech Assignments:

ASSIGNMENT	**Time Warp Speech**
OBJECTIVE	To present a short speech like you might be asked to give 5-10 years from now (or an *excerpt* from that speech)
TOPIC	Open, but don't give a speech about what you plan to do in 5-10 years, *be* yourself in 5-10 years delivering a speech somewhere.
SUPPORT	As needed.
TIME RANGE	2-3 minutes
DELIVERY STYLE	Appropriate for the imagined situation
NOTES	Note cards permitted, if appropriate for the imagined situation.
VISUAL AIDS	None
ATTIRE	Appropriate for the imagined situation
HINTS	Be creative. Aim high! Sample topics used by previous students include, "My Academy Award Acceptance Speech," "Arguing to the PTA to get a Stop Sign in Front of My House," and "Talking to a Second Grade Class about My Job."
ADDITIONAL INFORMATION	
MY SPEAKING DATE	_______________

ASSIGNMENT	**Speech Fear Speech**
OBJECTIVE	To share with the class your experiences with speech anxiety, including possible origins for the anxiety and your plan to overcome it
TOPIC	*You* are the topic.
SUPPORT	As needed
TIME RANGE	2-3 minutes
DELIVERY STYLE	Extemporaneous
NOTES	One note card permitted
VISUAL AIDS	None
HINTS	Don't be too tough on yourself. As you prepare, keep in mind that speech anxiety impacts a great majority of people.
ADDITIONAL INFORMATION	
MY SPEAKING DATE	_______________

Icebreaker Speech Assignments, cont'd.

ASSIGNMENT	**Introduction Speech**
OBJECTIVE	To interview a classmate for 5-10 minutes, learning information about his or her life experiences, then to introduce that person to the class as through he/she was about to be the guest speaker for the class today.
TOPIC	A classmate
SUPPORT	Facts, stories, explanations, and/or testimony from your classmate
TIME RANGE	60-90 seconds
DELIVERY STYLE	Extemporaneous
NOTES	One note card permitted
VISUAL AIDS	None
ATTIRE	Casual
HINTS	Don't be vague. Use interesting details. Make the person you will be introducing sound as interesting as possible.
ADDITIONAL INFORMATION	

MY SPEAKING DATE ________________

Impromptu Speech Assignments:

ASSIGNMENT	**Simple Topic Speech**
OBJECTIVE	To offer the audience insight or simple wisdom about your topic
TOPIC	A word or short phrase to be drawn randomly
SUPPORT	Personal experience and knowledge
TIME RANGE	2-3 minutes
DELIVERY STYLE	Impromptu
NOTES	One note card permitted
VISUAL AIDS	None
ATTIRE	Casual
HINTS	Don't let not knowing the topic overwhelm you. If you don't panic, the ideas will flow easily when you prepare.
ADDITIONAL INFORMATION	

MY SPEAKING DATE ________________

ASSIGNMENT	**Quotation-based Impromptu Speech**
OBJECTIVE	To offer the audience insight into a particular quotation or saying
TOPIC	A quotation to be drawn randomly in class (may be from a famous person, song, book, movie, etc.)
SUPPORT	Personal experience and knowledge
TIME RANGE	2-3 minutes
DELIVERY STYLE	Impromptu
NOTES	One note card permitted
VISUAL AIDS	None
ATTIRE	Casual
HINTS	Try to break the quotation down to a simple idea or phrase. It will make it easier to think of support.
ADDITIONAL INFORMATION	

MY SPEAKING DATE ________________

Impromptu Speech Assignments, cont'd:

ASSIGNMENT	**Impromptu Sales Speech**
OBJECTIVE	To persuade the audience to buy a product or service
TOPIC	Provided to you in class
SUPPORT	As needed
TIME RANGE	2-3 minutes
DELIVERY STYLE	Impromptu
NOTES	One note card permitted
VISUAL AIDS	None
ATTIRE	Casual
HINTS	Have fun and be creative!
ADDITIONAL INFORMATION	

MY SPEAKING DATE ______________

Informative Speech Assignments:

ASSIGNMENT Speech Introduction Speech
OBJECTIVE To perform and refine the introduction to your informative speech
TOPIC Your informative introduction
SUPPORT As needed
TIME RANGE 30-90 seconds
DELIVERY STYLE Extemporaneous
NOTES One note card permitted
VISUAL AIDS Only permitted if part of the introduction
ATTIRE Casual
HINTS Memorize at least the first line of your introduction so you can begin by looking at your audience for a whole thought.
ADDITIONAL INFORMATION

MY SPEAKING DATE ______________

ASSIGNMENT Informative Demonstration Speech
OBJECTIVE To teach your audience how to do something they probably do not already know how to do.
TOPIC Your choice
SUPPORT As needed
TIME RANGE 4-6 minutes
DELIVERY STYLE Extemporaneous
NOTES Two note cards permitted. Notes discouraged, as your hands will probably be busy.
VISUAL AIDS If appropriate for topic.
ATTIRE Casual
HINTS Food is great, but be sure to practice the whole speech with food preparation before you arrive. Unprepared demonstration speeches tend to go very overtime.
ADDITIONAL INFORMATION

MY SPEAKING DATE ______________

Informative Speech Assignments, cont'd

:

ASSIGNMENT **Informative Revelation Speech**

OBJECTIVE To organize, support, and deliver a researched informational speech.

TOPIC Should be something new and unique, but also relevant to your audience. Teach us something we did not know about before listening to your speech. See Sample Topic List in Appendix C for ideas.

SUPPORT Minimum of 6 sources must be cited during the speech. Sources must be current and credible.

TIME RANGE 5-8 minutes

DELIVERY STYLE Extemporaneous

NOTES Two note cards permitted with writing on one side only

VISUAL AIDS Ask instructor

ATTIRE Professional appearance

HINTS

ADDITIONAL INFORMATION

MY SPEAKING DATE ______________

ASSIGNMENT **Cultural Informative Speech**

OBJECTIVE To educate your audience about an unfamiliar culture or subculture, or an aspect of a culture.

TOPIC Your choice

SUPPORT Minimum of 5 sources to be cited in the speech, including 1 interview.

TIME RANGE 5-8 minutes for individual speech; 12-15 minutes for group presentation

DELIVERY STYLE Extemporaneous

NOTES Two note cards permitted with writing on one side only

VISUAL AIDS Ask instructor

ATTIRE Appropriate for topic

HINTS Dig deep. Avoid making stereotypical assumptions about a culture.

ADDITIONAL INFORMATION

MY SPEAKING DATE ______________

Persuasive Speech Assignments:

ASSIGNMENT	**Personal Action-Changing Persuasive Speech**
OBJECTIVE	To persuade your audience members to take a specific action or change a specific behavior
TOPIC	Your choice; avoid topics that are obvious or too difficult for audience members to accept
SUPPORT	Minimum 6 sources to be cited in the speech. Sources must be current and credible.
TIME RANGE	6-8 minutes
DELIVERY STYLE	Extemporaneous
NOTES	Two note cards permitted with writing on one side only
VISUAL AIDS	Optional
ATTIRE	Professional
HINTS	Be sure to include appeals to ethos, pathos, and logos.
ADDITIONAL INFORMATION	

MY SPEAKING DATE ______________

ASSIGNMENT	**Policy-Changing Persuasive Speech**
OBJECTIVE	To persuade your audience members that a government or organization should take a specific action and/or change an existing law or policy.
TOPIC	Your choice; avoid topics that are obvious or too difficult for audience members to accept
SUPPORT	Minimum 8 sources to be cited in the speech. Sources must be current and credible.
TIME RANGE	8-10 minutes
DELIVERY STYLE	Extemporaneous
NOTES	Two note cards permitted with writing on one side only
VISUAL AIDS	Optional
ATTIRE	Professional
HINTS	Be sure to include appeals to ethos, pathos, and logos. Choose a policy that has some impact on your audience.
ADDITIONAL INFORMATION	

MY SPEAKING DATE ______________

Persuasive Speech Assignments, cont'd:

ASSIGNMENT	**Monroe's Motivated Sequence Persuasive Speech**
OBJECTIVE	To persuade your audience members to take a specific action, change a specific behavior, or support a specific policy
TOPIC	Your choice; avoid topics that are obvious or too difficult for audience members to accept
SUPPORT	Minimum 6 sources to be cited in the speech. Sources must be current and credible.
TIME RANGE	6-8 minutes
DELIVERY STYLE	Extemporaneous
NOTES	Two note cards permitted with writing on one side only
VISUAL AIDS	Optional
ATTIRE	Professional
HINTS	Be sure to use all 5 steps of Monroe's Sequence. See Chapter 15 for details.
ADDITIONAL INFORMATION	

MY SPEAKING DATE ______________

ASSIGNMENT	**Group Sales Presentation**
OBJECTIVE	To develop a new product or service and seek financial backing from a corporate venture firm with a persuasive presentation
TOPIC	Your product and why they should give you money
SUPPORT	As needed
TIME RANGE	18-22 minutes
DELIVERY STYLE	Extemporaneous
NOTES	Two note cards permitted per group member with writing on one side only
VISUAL AIDS	Required
ATTIRE	Professional
HINTS	Make your presentation interactive. Don't just have each group member speak for 5 minutes in turn.
ADDITIONAL INFORMATION	

MY SPEAKING DATE ______________

Special Occasion Speech Assignments:

ASSIGNMENT	**Memorable Experience Speech**
OBJECTIVE	To organize and deliver a speech about a past experience
TOPIC	May be serious or humorous, but must be meaningful and vivid
SUPPORT	Your experience and observations
TIME RANGE	2-3 minutes
DELIVERY STYLE	Extemporaneous
NOTES	One note card (optional)
VISUAL AIDS	None
ATTIRE	Casual
HINTS	Consider these topic areas: most embarrassing moment; my longest minute; biggest surprise of my life; narrow escape; strangest coincidence.
ADDITIONAL INFORMATION	

MY SPEAKING DATE _______________

ASSIGNMENT	**Hero Speech**
OBJECTIVE	To thoughtfully write and revise a short speech commemorating someone who has been a personal hero in your life.
TOPIC	A specific person, not yourself
SUPPORT	Your own opinions and experiences
TIME RANGE	2-3 minutes
DELIVERY STYLE	Manuscript
NOTES	Manuscript
VISUAL AIDS	None
ATTIRE	Casual
HINTS	Be detailed and specific. Avoid clichés. Make delivery notes on your manuscript.
ADDITIONAL INFORMATION	

MY SPEAKING DATE _______________

Special Occasion Speech Assignments, cont'd:

ASSIGNMENT	**Pet Peeve Speech**
OBJECTIVE	To prepare and deliver a short speech about something that irritates you, and will also be of interest to your audience
TOPIC	Your choice
SUPPORT	Your opinions and experiences
TIME RANGE	2-3 minutes
DELIVERY STYLE	Manuscript
NOTES	Manuscript
VISUAL AIDS	None
ATTIRE	Casual
HINTS	Humor can be very effective. Make delivery notes on your manuscript.
ADDITIONAL INFORMATION	

MY SPEAKING DATE ______________

ASSIGNMENT	**Movie Review**
OBJECTIVE	To present a summary and review of a film
TOPIC	A film (Choose one that is not obvious or cliché.)
SUPPORT	Your opinions and a clip from the film
TIME RANGE	3-4 minutes
DELIVERY STYLE	Extemporaneous
NOTES	One note card per person
VISUAL AIDS	Required (short video clip)
ATTIRE	Casual and/or appropriate
HINTS	Remember why people read movie reviews – to decide if they want to see the film. Pick a film you think people probably haven't seen.
ADDITIONAL INFORMATION	

MY SPEAKING DATE ______________

Skill-Building Speech Assignments:

ASSIGNMENT	**Oral Interpretation**
OBJECTIVE	To perform a selection of poetry, fiction, or a scene from a play written by someone else
TOPIC	Literature
SUPPORT	None
TIME RANGE	2-3 minutes
DELIVERY STYLE	Manuscript
NOTES	Manuscript
VISUAL AIDS	None
ATTIRE	Casual, no costumes
HINTS	Choose a selection with lots of energy and interesting characters. Children's literature is very fun for this assignment.
ADDITIONAL INFORMATION	

MY SPEAKING DATE _______________

ASSIGNMENT	**Supporting Materials Speech**
OBJECTIVE	To support a single thesis/argument with at least five kinds of supporting materials
TOPIC	Your thesis
SUPPORT	Five different types
TIME RANGE	2-3 minutes
DELIVERY STYLE	Extemporaneous
NOTES	One note card with writing on one side only
VISUAL AIDS	If chosen as a type of support
ATTIRE	Casual
HINTS	
ADDITIONAL INFORMATION	

MY SPEAKING DATE _______________

Skill-Building Speech Assignments, con'td.

ASSIGNMENT	**Declamation**
OBJECTIVE	To perform a selection from a speech written by someone else
TOPIC	The speech
SUPPORT	None
TIME RANGE	3-4 minutes
DELIVERY STYLE	Manuscript
NOTES	Manuscript
VISUAL AIDS	None
ATTIRE	Casual
HINTS	Avoid very familiar speeches like "I Have a Dream." Your audience will be comparing your delivery to whomever gave that speech previously. See Appendix B for resources to find famous speeches.
ADDITIONAL INFORMATION	

MY SPEAKING DATE ________________

Sample Speeches

Sample Memorable Experience Speech Outline

INTRODUCTION

I. Attention Device: How many of you would place yourselves in a body of water several feet deep, with a dozen animals ranging from 5-7 feet long, weighing up to 400 pounds, who can swim up to 60 mph, and who have been known to kill sharks on their own?

II. Topic Revelation Statement: Today, I'll share with you the story of my dolphin swim nine months ago at the Dolphin Research Center in the Florida Keys.

BODY

I. Experience

A. The dolphin-swim lasted about 30 minutes, but we were at the facility three hours.
B. We sat in a classroom and received an informative talk about the facility and lessons on how to communicate with the dolphins.
C. We were led down to the docks and were introduced to the dolphins.
D. First we did something called "imitates."
E. The best part of all -- the actual dolphin-swim.

II. The Lesson to Be Learned

A. We can live in harmony with these beautiful, intelligent creatures.
B. It is crucial to their existence that we all do something to help protect them.
C. Purchase dolphin-safe tuna.
D. Cut up plastic rings that come on 6-packs of soda.

CONCLUSION

I. Review Statement: Now you know a bit about my amazing dolphin swim.

II. Lasting Thought: I strongly recommend this for anyone who is able. I even brought some information with me tonight so that you may plan your own underwater adventure!

Sample Hero Speech Manuscript

If you asked him, he'd tell you that he never really liked teaching, or teenagers, or anything, really. Most of the other kids in my class called him words like grouch, or grinch, or a lot worse. Even I didn't like him for a long time – especially how he always smelled like Switzer Sweet cheap cigars. But, by the end of 11th grade, Mr. Largent turned out to be the most important and influential teacher I ever had. I'd like to tell you why I consider him to be a hero in my life.

Classic Literature is pretty far from the mind of your average teenager, and that's who I was at the start of 11th grade. I didn't have a care in the world, except for what kind of car I would buy as soon as I could save the money. Third period was English Lit with Mr. Largent, and while he would mumble aloud from Homer, we'd all pass notes and watch the clock. Sometimes he'd try to get us involved or excited about the book we were reading, which for most of the term was *The Odyssey*, but the tide was definitely against him in that classroom. Sometimes I felt sorry for him and pretended to listen, but I never thought to let him actually enter my mind and make any additions or improvements. And then one day he just snuck right in.

At the end of The Odyssey, the main character Odysseus comes home to his wife after being gone for years. While he was gone he wasn't exactly faithful, either. For our final assignment of the class, Mr. Largent asked us to write something different than we'd done before. He wanted us to think about our own lives and write about someone who may have left us for a period during our lives – even for a short time – and how we felt about them coming back. I thought about writing about my dog, Bo, who left when I was in sixth grade, but I couldn't. My hand just started writing about my dad.

He left me and my mom when I was a Freshman and never came back. He had only called twice since, and other than that we just heard about him from people we knew, kind of like Odysseus. What was supposed to be a three page paper was becoming a twelve page paper as I wrote and wrote. I argued first that the wife should not take him back for any reason, and then that he should never have come home at all. But by the end, through tears, I decided that she'd take him, of course, just like we'd take my Dad if he ever showed up again. As embarrassing or humiliating as it might be, you want the person more than your pride. And after I wrote my paper, I wrote my Dad a letter telling him that I always hoped he'd be a part of my life, and that he could always come back to me, and that I hope he does.

I haven't heard from my Dad yet, but I got a really wonderful note on my paper from Mr. Largent. He said that my essay was one of the best he's ever had, and that he was glad that an ancient story could still mean something to a teenage girl today. I know it doesn't seem like a lot, but Mr. Largent made me realize that everyone has something to teach us, and that we should always learn things that are presented to us in school – because you never know when it will suddenly jump out of the past and hit home.

Sample Impromptu Speech Outline

Topic: "Keep true to the dreams of thy youth." (Schiller)

Introduction

I. Attention Device: What do Bill Clinton, Oksana Baiul and Tom Hanks have in common?

II. Topic Revelation: "Keep true to the dreams of thy youth."

III. Preview of Main Points: Today we will examine three individuals who made the dreams from their youth come true. First, in politics, we will discuss Bill Clinton. Next, in the arena of sports, we will see how Oksana Bauil made her ice skating dream come true. Finally, we will look to the world of entertainment and discover how Tom Hanks was able to fulfill his dream.

Body

I. Bill Clinton met President Kennedy when he visited the White House as a young man. On that day, he decided he would be President of the United States.

II. Oksana Bauil, as a young child in Russia, wanted to be a figure skater. Even though she had much hardship, including the loss of her parents, she didn't quit. One day, she found herself on the victory stand at the Olympic Games.

III. Tom Hanks saw a play when he was young. He was amazed that people earned their living acting and on the spot decided that he would do the same.

Conclusion

I. Review of Topic and Main Points: I have discussed the topic, "Keep true to the dreams of thy youth." We saw how Bill Clinton in politics, Oksana Bauil in sports, and Tom Hanks in entertainment didn't lose sight of their childhood dreams.

II. Lasting Thought: The next time you are asked what do Bill Clinton, Oksana Bauil, and Tom Hanks have in common, you will know that it is that they persisted and made their dreams come true.

Sample Demonstration Speech Outline

Specific Purpose: To inform my audience about how to make throw pillows.
Topic Revelation Statement: Today I will show you how to make your own easy and attractive throw pillows.

Introduction

I. Attention Device: Last week I was in Pottery Barn and they had some gorgeous throw pillows made of velvet. I was going to get them until I saw the price -- $60 each. I couldn't afford it, so I did the next best thing – and now I'll show you how to do that, too.

II. Topic Revelation Statement: Today I will show you how to make your own easy and attractive throw pillows.

III. Significance Statement: Even if you are on a budget, you can still have a home that reflects your taste and style. Your home says a lot about who you are.

IV. Preview of Main Points: First we'll go over the items you'll need, then we'll make the pillow case, and then we'll finish the pillow.

Body

I. First, you should assemble the items you will need.

- A. You'll need to go to a fabric or craft store for most of the items.
  - 1. I recommend an upholstery store for better fabrics.
  - 2. Purchase ¾ yards of fabric for each pillow you want.
  - 3. Purchase a pillow insert, approximately 14 inches square.
    - a. If you have an old pillow you can use its stuffing.
    - b. I always use new inserts because I have allergies.
- B. Also – you'll need thread and a needle or a sewing machine.

II. Now that you have your supplies, we can make the case.

- A. Fold your fabric in half and iron it.
- B. Measure a square 3 inches taller and wider than your pillow insert. Pin the fabric together and trim.<Show pinning and cutting.>
- C. Turn the fabric inside out.
- D. Sew along the edges about ½ inch from the edge. Leave a small opening on one side in the center. <Show sample with hole.>
- E. Stick your fingers in the opening and turn it inside out. The good side of the fabric should be showing now.

continued

III. Now that you have a case, you can finish the pillow.

A. Stuff the insert or the stuffing into the opening. <Do this.>
B. Stitch the opening closed with a matching thread.
C. Shape the pillow <Show how to do this.>

Conclusion

I. Review Topic and Main Points: Now you know how to make a throw pillow. You learned about the items you need, how to make a case, and how to finish it.

II. Lasting Thought: So don't just look at designer home fashions and dream. Spend a few minutes and make your own fabulous accessories!

Sample Informative Revelation Speech Outline

Specific Purpose: to educate my classmates about new research on saliva
Topic Revelation Statement: New research is being conducted on saliva, with potentially life-saving results.

INTRODUCTION

I. Attention Getter: In 1903, Dr. Ivan Pavlov published his groundbreaking research in which he conditioned dogs to salivate on cue by ringing a bell. As far as most of you are concerned, this is probably the most interesting research ever conducted involving saliva. Dr. Irwin Mandel said it best when he stated, "Saliva doesn't have the drama of blood, the integrity of sweat or the emotional appeal of tears." But it's time for people to start paying attention to the forgotten bodily fluid – saliva.

II. Central Idea: New research is being conducted on saliva, with potentially life-saving results.

III. Significance Statement: *The Los Angeles Times of January 21, 2002* reports that over 25 million Americans suffer from saliva deficiency, with potentially disastrous consequences for your mouth, teeth, and breath. What scientists are discovering about saliva could have wide spread benefits in everything from fixing bad breath to preventing AIDS.

IV. Preview: First, we'll uncover some of the basic facts about saliva. Then, we'll investigate some saliva related problems. Finally, we'll turn our attention to some promising saliva research that'll have you drooling.

BODY

I. There are many interesting facts about saliva.

- A. Let's begin by defining saliva.
  - 1. Saliva is a complex secretion formed mainly from the salivary glands.
    - a. According to a brochure published by the *American Academy of Otolaryngology,* titled *Salivary Glands: What's Normal, What's Abnormal,* we have hundreds of salivary glands in our throats and mouths.
    - b. The major glands are located near the upper teeth, in front of the tongue, and on the floor of the mouth.
    - c. *The Augusta Chronicle of September 11, 2001* reports that these glands can produce up to 3 pints of saliva per day.
  - 2. Saliva is mostly water, but *Hormonal Update in a story posted on October 19, 2001,* notes that saliva also contains hundreds of enzymes, proteins, minerals, blood cells, and bacteria.

B. Saliva is one of the body's most important fluids.
   1. *Chemist and Druggist of March 31, 2001* explains that saliva is like your body's natural mouthwash.
      a. It protects your mouth by neutralizing acidic foods.
      b. It sweeps away bacteria that cause cavities and tooth decay.
   2. The previously cited *Los Angeles Times* reports that saliva also eases digestion, prevents bad breath, and makes speaking easier.

C. Saliva was once viewed negatively.
   1. Centuries ago, doctors believed that saliva contained evil spirits released by the brain.
   2. They would also poison patients with mercury to cause saliva to pour out of patients' mouths.

II. There are a several common problems associated with saliva.

A. It is possible to have too much saliva.
   1. *The Practitioner of October 12, 2001* points out that there are a small number of people who suffer from sialorrhoea, or "excessive saliva production."
   2. Sialorrhoea is caused by menstruation, early pregnancy, weakening of mouth muscles from Parkinson's disease, epilepsy, and other disorders.

B. A total lack of saliva is also possible.
   1. *The August 13, 2001 Chattanooga Times* explains that Sjogren's syndrome is an illness in which the body's immune system attacks and destroys the salivary glands.
   2. The cause of Sjogren's syndrome is still not known, but is currently being researched.
   3. Sufferers of Sjogren's syndrome often use artificial saliva.
      a. The previously cited *Chemist and Druggist* claims that it mimics the feel of saliva.
      b. However, it is missing the proteins and enzymes that real saliva provides.

C. Xerostomia, or dry mouth, is the most common saliva disorder.
   1. *According to the Pittsburgh Post Gazette of March 21, 2000* xerostomia is a side effect of more than 500 prescription drugs including anti-depressants, anti-histamines and acne medications.
   2. Dr. Athena Pappa, Professor at Tufts University School of Dental Medicine notes that people with dry mouth have ten times the normal amount of bacteria in their mouths.
   3. *The Ayr Advocate of August 9, 2000* says that dry mouth sufferers are turning to water, candies, and sugarless gums to return their saliva production to normal.

III. There is a great deal of new research about saliva.

A. Saliva is being used in law enforcement.
   1. The British government, according to the *February 19, 2001 Press Association,*

says that saliva is more reliable and convenient than blood for testing.

2. A pamphlet on saliva by *National Institute of Dental and Craniofacial Research* points out that saliva contains pieces of your DNA.
    a. A few drops can reveal whether you've had too much to drink or have been using illegal drugs.
    b. Dried saliva on a postage stamp or envelope can even be used to identify who sent a letter.

B. Saliva's proteins are being isolated and used to create new drugs.
1. Scientists were inspired by animals licking their wounds.
    a. *Beyond 2000 of March 14, 2001* says that researchers have discovered a new protein in saliva called secretory leukocyte protease inhibitor, or SLPI.
    b. SLPI can accelerate the healing of wounds.
    c. This research is being used to develop treatments for patients with non-healing wounds and for day-to-day cuts and scrapes.
2. Scientists have also discovered the protein histatin.
    a. *The May 1, 2001 Drug Discovery and Technology News* says that histatin is being used against oral lesions associated with HIV.
    b. *PR Newswire of January 8, 2002* also reports that histatin is being tested against viral infections associated with cystic fibrosis.
3. Finally, *a January 7, 1998 press release from the Cornell University Medical College* reports that they are focusing on a component of saliva that blocks HIV growth and are working on a drug that prevents HIV transmission.

CONCLUSION

I. Review of Topic and Main Points: Now you know some of the basic facts about saliva, some saliva related problems, and the latest research on the matter.

II. Lasting Thought: Ivan Pavlov did produce one of the most famous psychological discoveries of all time, but that was not what he set out to do. Pavlov was a biologist, and his famous experiment began as an attempt to understand how saliva helped dogs digest food. One hundred years later, scientists are still learning more about the fascinating properties of saliva. Sure it sounds gross, but try getting through a speech without it.

WORKS CITED

Barrett, David. "Police to Pilot Saliva Drug Test." *Press Association* 19 Feb. 2001.

Casano, Peter, ed. "Salivary Glands: What's Normal, What's Abnormal." American Academy of Otolaryngology. 2002 <http://www.sinuscarecenter.com/salivaao.html>.

"Demgen Scientists Publish Antibacterial Activity of P113D Against Cystic Fibrosis Infections." *PR Newswire* 8 Jan. 2002. Lexis-Nexis.

Donohue, Paul. "A Life Without Saliva and Tears is Miserable." *Chattanooga Times* 13 Aug. 2001: D4.

"Dry Mouth Can Lead to Tooth Decay." *Ayr Advocate* 9 Aug. 2000: 14.

"Histatin Tested Against Candidiasis." *Drug Discovery & Technology News* 4.5 (2001).

McIntosh, Shirley. "Physical, Mental Conditions Can Aggravate Dry Mouth." *Augusta Chronicle* 11 Sept. 2001: A15.

Mestel, Rosie. "The Gland Tour: How Saliva is Made." *Los Angeles Times* 21 Jan. 2002: S6.

Mestel, Rosie. "The Wonders of Saliva." *Los Angeles Times* 21 Jan. 2002: S1+.

"National Institute for Dental and Craniofacial Research." American Dental Education Association. 2000 <http://www.adea.org/CPPA_Materials/Factsheets/2002NIDCR.pdf>

Parker-Pope, Tara. "Is Your Mouth as Dry as a Desert?" *Pittsburgh Post-Gazette* 21 March 2000: C4+.

"Salivary Hormone Monitoring." Hormonal Update 2.1 (2001): 13 pars. 19 Oct. 2001 <http://www.aeron.com/volume_2_number_1.htm>

Sung, Peggy. "Study Shows Component of Saliva is Very Effective in Blocking AIDS Virus." Weill Medical College of Cornell University. 7 Jan. 1998 <http://www.nycornell.org/news/press/1998/saliva.aids.html>

"The Gob-I Desert." *Chemist and Druggist* 31 March 2001: 25+.

"The Role of Saliva in Oral Health Problems." *The Practitioner* 12 Oct. 2001: 841+.

"Tongue Bath." Beyond 2000 14 Mar. 2001 <http://www.beyond2000.com/news/Oct_00/story_805.html>

Sample Informative Revelation Speech Manuscript
World's Fairs by Tyler Adams, 2000

Introduction

This year, the world focused its attention on one city for a global event that brought together 156 of earth's nations. This multi-billion dollar undertaking was attended by millions of people from all corners of the globe. You probably read about it in newspapers and magazines, and saw it on TV - unless you live in the U.S. No, I'm not giving a speech about the Olympics - heaven knows we've had our fill of Bob Costas. The event I'm talking about is Expo 2000 – the most recent World's Fair held this June through October in Hanover, Germany.

For 150 years World's Fairs have showcased the most amazing and far-reaching cultural and technological advances - just like an informative round...but on a slightly grander scale. According to the *Bangkok Post of August 13, 2000* attending the World's Fair is like traveling ahead in time. Since 1851, nearly a billion people have seen the future at a world exposition. Yet we may not realize the staggering impact they have had and are still having. That's where I come in.

Today I'll first take you back in time and examine the history of International Expositions. Next measure the impacts past World's Fairs have had on our present. Finally I'll take you on a brief tour of the future, as was unfolded at Expo 2000 and consider the U.S. government's shocking decision not to participate.

First Main Point

Some say that the World's Fairs were in a way the first real Internet. Not in the computer sense – but in the way they drew millions to a common space occupied by people from around the world sharing the most advanced technologies, ideas and culture – with global impacts. The first World's Fair, held in London in 1851, focused on one main exhibition hall, the still standing Crystal Palace. Over 17 thousand exhibitors demonstrated their world wide wares.

The Fair was conceived by English nobleman Sir Henry Cole, ostensibly to promote harmony among all the peoples of the world. but Erik Mattie notes in his 1998 sociological overview, *World's Fairs*, that the market exposure the fair provided for British products was also a strong motivating factor. Over the nest few fairs, though, public attendance grew and the focus shifted. New products were still featured but it was now their entertainment value that was paramount. This increased importance of entertainment was evident in the 1893 Chicago World's Fair which saw the advent of a separate amusement area featuring the world's first ever Ferris Wheel. And as the turn of the century...turned, and official body was organized to govern universal expositions. Since 1931, the Bureau International des Expositions, BIE for short, has established the dates and locations of World's Fairs. There is no set time interval between fairs. Sometimes years go by without a fair, and sometimes multiple fairs are held in the same year. This was the case in 1939, when the seminal New York World's Fair was held at the same time as an International Exposition hosted by San Francisco to celebrate the completion of the Golden Gate Bridge.

There is no questioning the popularity of World's Fairs - even the first one in 1851 drew an attendance of over 6 million people and was participated in by 28 countries. While attendance to fairs has varied over the decades according to locations and the political and economic environment at the time, recent expositions have garnered as many as 64 million visitors and involved as many as 156 nations. World's Fairs provide unique opportunities to the hosting location, such as increased tourism and outlandish, but inescapable, hotel rates. The host can also benefit culturally. The Architectural Record of this July notes that Expo 2000 was also intended to encourage Germans to be more tolerant of foreigners. A noble goal…if only Germany had pursued it back in the '30s.

World's Fairs do not only affect their hosts. Let's move on and see how they impact the whole world.

Second Main Point

<Show visual #1> These distinctive structures may look familiar to you, but do you know where they are? Ok, it's a trick question. The Trylon and Perisphere, theme buildings of the 1939 World's Fair were demolished soon after the fairs closing. This is the case with most World's Fair structures – they are meant to last only a short while. World's Fairs, like time, are fleeting – if you don't see them during their run, you never will. But there are occasional survivors.

<Visual #2> The Unisphere, built for the 1964 expo, now stands on the exact same ground once occupied by the Trylon and Perisphere. Another surviving, and frankly butt-ugly, structure is the nearby watchtowers <Visual #3>, which you may have seen almost crush Will Smith in the movie "Men in Black." So close, but yet, so far. Across the country is Seattle's most distinctive landmark. The Space Needle <Visual #4> did not, contrary to popular belief, fall from space. It was constructed from the ground up for the 1964 World's Fair. The U.S. pavilion at Expo '67 took the form of a giant geodesic dome <Visual #5>. While most Americans have never seen this Montreal landmark, you might be familiar with its evil clone at Disney's Epcot Center, itself an evil clone of the 1939 New York World's Fair.

Paris, France. City of Lights…City of Love. It's most famous landmark: <Visual #6> La Tour Eiffel – built not out of love but for, say it with me, the World's Fair, this one in 1889. Arguably the world's most recognizable edifice, the Tower was also intended as a temporary structure. Strange as it may seem this landmark was originally thought to be unsightly and even monstrous by artists, architects, and those picky Parisians. The fact that the tower is now looked on as a symbol of French national pride is evidence of Gustave Eiffel's triumph of innovative design, and also bears testament to the ability of World's Fairs to reshape our perception of the world.

Culture and art have also been influenced by World's Fairs. Since Amsterdam in 1883, the fairs have featured exhibits of both contemporary and historical societies from around the world. For those of us who are more likely to participate in less intellectual – and more tasty – aspects of culture, it is interesting to note that Belgian waffles, iced tea (the beverage, not the rapper), and the ice cream cone all made their debut at World's Fairs. While the world waits for contact from space aliens, the first contact the common man made with extraterrestrial matter was at...the World's Fair. In Osaka in 1970 the public was able to experience a new aspect of culture by visiting a moon rock exhibit.

By far, the most influential aspect of World's Fairs has been in the area of technology. In the days before the Discovery Channel, World's Fairs provided a way for people to experience future innovations that were not yet attainable to the average person. The elevator, the escalator, the sewing machine, and even the Ford Mustang all premiered at World's Fairs, as did false teeth and artificial limbs. However, the types of inventions that have been the most notable are those dealing with communications – now that seems relevant. Ever since the telegraph was demonstrated at the inaugural fair in London, World's Fairs have showcased the next step in electronic communication. That's right, television, which has had at least a slight global impact, made its public debut at the 1939 New York World's Fair, and I think you'll agree with me that the world has never been the same.

Third Main Point

OK class, let's review. World's Fairs are huge, popular, and important. So why after 150 years of participation was the U.S. a no-show in Hannover? Before we answer that question, let's look at what Expo 2000 was all about. The *Malaysia Business Times, August 14, 2000* says that the expo aimed to "open people's minds to issues, ideas, visions, and concepts which can help mankind respond to the challenges of the new millennium."

According to the *June 1, 2000 Irish Times*, the fair grounds were rather large -- about the same size as Monaco - that's a lot of space. The most popular sites at Expo 2000 included the Japanese pavilion which was made out of recyclable paper, and the Dutch pavilion which looked like some kind of huge club sandwich with a live forest in the middle. Entertainers at the fair included Carlos Santana and Britney Spears.

Expo 2000 came under criticism from the international press because it failed to reach, or even come close to, its projected attendance of 40 million. However, the *Jakarta Post of September 7, 2000* points out that the problem was with the unrealistic projection, not with attendance. Expo 2000 was also criticized on *October 8, 2000 by the New Zealand paper The Dominion* for losing money, and The *Scotsman of this September 6th* claimed that it was such a bomb that the 2,000 prostitutes who came to town for the event gave up and went home.

It's important to note though, that World's Fairs have historically lost money. World's Fairs aren't organized to make a profit, they are put on to promote cooperation, harmony, and the future. Sadly – for the US – it came down to money. *U.S. News and World Report of June 5, 2000* explains that after expensive Expos in '92 and '98 , Congress passed a law disallowing the use of tax dollars for World's Fairs. They expected corporate sponsors to front the money, but the Fortune 500 didn't bite. Consequently, impoverished Ethiopia had a presence at the Expo but, according to the *San Diego Union-Tribune July, 30 2000* with just weeks before opening and a huge

Pavilion space reserved in the center of the Fair – we bailed out. The only presence the wealthiest nation on earth had was through commercial ventures like IBM, McDonald's, and Microsoft.

According to the *Baltimore Sun of July 12, 2000* US non-participation conveyed all kinds of messages to the world – none of them positive. It may even partially explain our negative trade balance. At a minimum, it says that we *aren't* the world.

Also as a result of our non-participation, very few Americans attended and there was almost no media coverage of this enormous global event in US media. So did we miss anything?

>The first live interaction between humans and a colony of Artificial Intelligence machines.
>The first public German apology for the holocaust and a memorial to its victims
>A scientifically-based projection of all major technological breakthroughs expected in the next 100 years and theories about their cultural and environmental impacts.

So in answer to my earlier question, YES, you missed A LOT. And that's just a sampling. There's no way I could tell you about everything at the expo in 10 minutes. Remember, it's the SIZE of MONACO. If you would like more information on Expo 2000, surf on over to www.expo2000.de where you can take an interactive tour of the Fair that was.

Conclusion

Today we have looked back at the history of World's Fairs, examined the effects they have had on our present, and taken a glimpse of the future represented by Expo 2000.

The most sought after collectible from the 1939 World's Fair is a lapel pin that proclaimed: "I have seen the future." The next World's Fair is slated for 2005 in Seto, Japan. Whether or not the US chooses to participate, I have no doubts that people who attend will once again see the future.

<Editor's Note: This is a speech that was written in manuscript form and memorized for use in intercollegiate forensics (speech) competitions. Tyler performed this speech in Prague, Czech Republic and won the International Championship for Informative Speaking in March 2001.>

Sample Persuasive Speech Outline: Problem/Cause/Solution

Specific Purpose: to influence my audience to pull over for emergency vehicles
Topic Revelation Statement: Today, I will argue that the lives of emergency workers and victims of accidents are seriously endangered by people who do not pull over for emergency vehicles.

INTRODUCTION

I. Attention Getter: February 22, 2002. Paramedics rush to the scene of an accident in Bucks County, Pennsylvania. In route, their ambulance is hit by a car flying through an intersection. According to the *August 6, 2002 Journal of Emergency Medical Services,* the ambulance rolled over onto a stopped car, injuring both people in the car and the paramedics in the ambulance. Sounds like a freak accident, but it turns out that the failure to yield to emergency vehicles is all too common.

II. Topic Revelation Statement: Today, I will argue that the lives of emergency workers and victims of accidents are seriously endangered by people who do not pull over for emergency vehicles.

III. Significance Statement: The consequences of our failure to pull over can often be deadly. *The Hamilton Spectator, February 25, 2002,* reports that until the deaths of firefighters at the World Trade Center on September 11th, 40 percent of all US firefighters killed in the line of duty were killed in vehicles on their way to the scene.

IV. Preview: First, I will explain to you why the failure to yield is a serious problem. Then, I will uncover why drivers aren't pulling over for emergency vehicles. Finally, I will develop some solutions to protect both drivers and our emergency workers.

BODY

I. The failure to yield to emergency vehicles is a serious problem.

- A. The problem is large and widespread.
  1. *The Deseret News of August 4, 2001* notes that nearly one out of five emergency calls is delayed by other drivers.
  2. Additionally, *The Memphis Commercial Appeal on December 31, 2001* called the failure to yield to emergency vehicles the most broken law in America.
- B. There are several ways motorists fail to yield.
  1. Motorists do not pull over to the side of the road or do not pull over so emergency vehicles can pass.
  2. *The Tampa Tribune of February 24, 2001* also reports that some drivers speed up or race ambulances and police cars.

a. Drivers may try to pass them.
b. Some emergency personnel tell stories of drivers who have made rude gestures toward them.

C. The failure to yield has serious consequences.
1. Many people are injured in accidents involving emergency vehicles.
a. *Best's Review of July 1, 2001* claims that there are more than 32,000 accidents each year involving emergency vehicles and civilians.
b. More than 17,000 injuries and hundreds of deaths are the result of these accidents.
c. *USA Today on March 21, 2002* noted that ambulances are 13 times more likely to be involved in an accident than a passenger vehicle.
2. Accidents also affect the people the emergency vehicles were going to save.
a. The previously cited *Deseret News* says that vehicles that don't pull over can cause a delay of 10 to 30 seconds.
b. Salt Lake Fire Captain Joe Ziolkowski states, "That time can add up quickly when dealing with a fast moving fire or a person who has stopped breathing. The brain only has a four-minute supply of oxygen reserve."

II. The failure to yield to emergency vehicles has several causes.

A. One reason people do not pull over is that they are unaware of emergency vehicles.
1. Distractions in cars like CD players, cell phones, and GPS systems often make drivers oblivious to what's around them.
2. A poll in the *Minneapolis Star Tribune of May 19, 2002* revealed that 60 percent of the motorists surveyed admitted that they do not notice ambulances until the last second.

B. Another reason people do not pull over is rudeness.
1. *The Bridgewater Courier News of October 6, 2002* states, "Firefighters complain a lack of courtesy has caused them to sit in traffic even though their trucks have their sirens blaring and their lights flashing."
2. Some motorists try to outrun ambulances or follow fire trucks to see what an accident looks like.

C. The biggest reason people do not pull over is confusion about how to react to an approaching vehicle.
1. Some motorists don't know they are supposed to pull over.
2. Others stop in the middle of intersections or panic and freeze because they don't know where to go.
a. In the previously cited *Star Tribune,* Mary Zappetillo wrote that while on her way to an emergency call, the ambulance she was driving was completely blocked because a driver refused to go through a red light to let her through.
b. Mary stated, "I had to put my vehicle in park and walk up and knock on his window to ask him to go through the intersection."
3. People don't know how to respond to flashing lights that aren't red.

a. Volunteers use blue lights on their vehicles.
b. Bethel Park Fire Chief Dan Moore explained to the previously cited *Best's Review,* "a lot of people don't know what those blue lights mean."

III. The failure to yield to emergency vehicles has some simple solutions.

A. One step in changing laws governing driver behavior around emergency vehicles.
1. The previously cited *Commercial Appeal*, reports that Illinois has passed a new statute known as Scott's Law.
a. Motorists who fail to yield to emergency vehicles are subject to automatic license suspension.
b. They may also receive up to a $10,000 fine.
2. Other laws allow paramedics to take down the license plate numbers of drivers that refuse to yield.
a. These drivers then receive traffic tickets via mail.
b. Three states have passed such laws.

B. *The Milwaukee Journal Sentinel of April 22, 2002* also notes that some communities are equipping emergency vehicles and traffic lights with devices that allow fire trucks and ambulances to turn all signal lights in an eight-block area red to clear their routes.

C. The biggest responsibility lies in making ourselves and others aware of some basic safety tips for yielding to emergency vehicles. These tips are from the previously cited *San Francisco Chronicle.*
1. Pull to the nearest edge of the road, even if it is to the left, and come to a complete stop.
2. Use turn signals so the drivers of the emergency vehicles know you are aware of their presence.
3. Keep the volume of your radio at a level where you can still hear sounds outside the car.
4. Never block an intersection.
5. Don't follow vehicles responding to an emergency at closer than 500 feet.
6. Pull over for all flashing lights, even if they are not red.

CONCLUSION

I. Review of Topic and Main Points: You have just learned about the threat of people not yielding to emergency vehicles. First, we examined the problem of drivers not pulling over for emergency vehicles. Then, we looked at why drivers do not yield. Finally, we have discussed some solutions to increase the safety of us and our emergency personnel.

II. Lasting Thought: The next time you see flashing lights in your rearview mirror, don't panic. Just ease over to the nearest shoulder. Remember that a life can be saved or lost in a matter of seconds.

WORKS CITED

Blake, Laurie. "Making Way for the Ambulance." *Minneapolis Star Tribune* 19 May 2002: 3B.

Davis, Robert. "Speeding to the Rescue Can Have Deadly Results." *USA Today* 21 Mar. 2002: 1A+.

Fabiano, Giovanni. "Emergency Workers Spreading the Word About Safety." *Bridgewater Courier News* 6 Oct. 2002: 1B.

Ford, Dave. "S.F. Drivers Can't Seem to Get Out of the Way of Emergency Vehicles." *The San Francisco Chronicle* 12 Apr. 2002: 1+.

Goch, Lynna. "Answering the Call; Emergency Vehicle Accidents Prove Costly for Insurers." *Best's Review* 102.3 (2001): 87.

Kelley, Dave. "Emergency Vehicle Crashes Around the World." *Journal of Emergency Medical Services* 6 August 2002 <http://www.jems.com/jems/news02/0806d.html>

Longbottom, Ross. "Warning, Emergency Vehicle Approaching." *The Hamilton Spectator* 25 Feb. 2002: D10.

"Most-Broken Law May Be Motorists' Failure to Yield to Emergency Vehicles." *The Commercial Appeal* 31 Dec. 2001: DS5.

Reavy, Pat. "Hear Firetruck Siren? Pull Over." *Deseret News* 4 Aug. 2001: A9.

Samolinski, Candace. "Device Clears the Way for Emergency Vehicles." *Tampa Tribune* 24 Feb. 2001: 1+.

Sandler, Larry. "Here's a Way To Change Those Silly Stoplights." *Milwaukee Journal Sentinel* 22 Apr. 2002: 2B.

Sample Persuasive Speech Outline: Monroe's Motivated Sequence

Specific Purpose: to persuade my classmates to support efforts to get students involved as election poll workers.

Topic Revelation Statement: With a national shortage of qualified poll workers and the growing presence of technology in elections, college and high school students are an untapped resource of election workers.

INTRODUCTION

I. Attention Getter: Hanging chads. Butterfly ballots. Recounts. These are words most Americans didn't know prior to the 2000 presidential election, but are very aware of now. As the Florida recount dragged on for nearly a month, Americans also learned a great deal about the flaws in our voting process. Counting errors, confusing ballots, and polling places that opened late and closed early were just a few of the issues that prompted calls for voting reforms. An issue that has remained for Florida and the rest of the states, though, is the difficulty of getting qualified people to work elections to cut down on errors.

II. Topic Revelation Statement: In fact, with a national shortage of qualified poll workers and the growing presence of technology in elections, college and high school students are an untapped resource of election workers. Today, I hope to persuade you to become part of the solution.

III. Significance Statement: Beverly Moore, director of the Warren County Board of Elections, told *The Cincinnati Enquirer of September 29, 2002*, "It seems like there should be a better way. The bottom line is poll workers are the backbones of elections."

IV. Preview: To see how we all can strengthen this backbone, let's first examine the need for more qualified poll workers. Second, we'll examine the plan to have more students working elections. Finally, I'll help you visualize the benefits of increased student participation in elections.

BODY

I. The current system for recruiting poll workers is failing. (NEED)

  A. There is a severe poll worker shortage.

    1. According to *The Sarasota Herald-Tribune of November 1, 2002,* there is difficulty finding poll workers because they have to work 14 hour days and are paid very little.

2. The results, according to the *previously cited Cincinnati Enquirer*, are that "mixed in with dedicated people...you get a lot of warm bodies that have no business being there."
3. Poll workers also often quit if they are confused or if trouble arises.

B. The shortage of qualified poll workers creates several problems.
1. According to *The Washington Post, September 14, 2002,* polling places open late if workers don't show up and have to close early if people quit.
2. Additionally, lack of familiarity with computerized voting systems affects voters.
    a. *The Chronicle of Higher Education on December 13, 2002,* notes that the typical poll worker is about 70, and intimidated by computers. They may leave if they get frustrated.
    b. This can lead to delays and errors in both voting and counting votes.

II. There is a large untapped source of poll workers available. (SATISFACTION)

A. Local governments should allow and encourage high school and college students to work polls.
1. *The Washington Post of August 29, 2002* notes that most students will work for the $6 per hour a poll worker is paid, and don't mind putting in a 14 hour day.
2. Students may also volunteer to receive community service credit at their high schools or colleges.
3. Most students have basic computer skills and familiarity with technology.

B. States will need to amend their laws to permit younger workers.
1. The previously cited *Washington Post* reports that most states require poll workers to be over 18 and registered voters.
2. 18 states, however, have lowered their requirements to allow 16 and 17-year old students to work polls in some capacity.
3. The previously cited *Cincinnati Enquirer* also claims that some states have instituted minimum GPA requirements to make sure they are getting the best students for their workers.

III. Student poll workers are an easily workable solution. (VISUALIZATION)

A. Several states and communities have already successfully implemented this policy.
1. Don Samuels, member of a voting task force, estimated in the *Sun-Sentinel of September 21, 2002,* that thousands of high school seniors would be helping out during the 2002 Florida elections.
2. Long Beach, California has allowed 16 and 17-year old students to serve as poll workers since 1997 with great success.

B. Bringing students into politics can help reduce student apathy.
1. Students are unlikely to participate in politics.
    a. According to *The Saint Louis Post-Dispatch on January 10, 2002* the percentage of 18-year olds voting reached its lowest level ever in the 2000 election.

    b. *The Daily Princetonian on December 9, 2002,* claims that a recent survey indicates students would rather do community service than get involved in politics.
2. Jane Elmes-Crahall, a professor of communications at Wilkes University, told the *San Bernardino Sun of November 7, 2002,* that students care very passionately about issues, but are disconnected from the political process.
3. Working at polls helps reconnect students with politics.
    a. Students can witness our democratic process in action.
    b. They can also read about relevant issues for the election in which they work.
    c. R. Michael Alvarez, professor of political science at Caltech, told the previously cited *Chronicle of Higher Education* that bringing students to the polls will have a long-term impact on their involvement in the political process.

CONCLUSION

I. Review of Topic and Main Points: We have seen the dramatic need for new poll workers by first understanding the shortage of qualified workers. Then, we noted that students represent an untapped source of election officials. Finally, we discovered that this process has the potential to revitalize youth participation in politics and has already experienced some success.

II. Call to Action: That's where we come in. As college students, we have the unique opportunity to inform ourselves about the political process and serve our communities. So consider the following actions. Volunteer in your precinct for the next election. Recruit friends, family, and fraternity, sorority, and club members to help, also. If younger students are not allowed to work polls where you live, lobby to have those laws changed.

III. Lasting Thought: The right to vote for 18-year olds was a hard fought battle. It's time we proved that we can make a valuable contribution to the political process.

WORKS CITED

Binette, Chad. "Florida's Poll Workers' Jobs Getting Tougher." *Sarasota Herald-Tribune* 1 Nov. 2002: BS1+.

Blunt, Matt & Tirozzi, Gerald. "Young Workers Could Solve Poll Problems." *St. Louis Post-Dispatch* 10 Jan. 2002: B7.

Huriash, Lisa. "Voting Task Force Enlists Students, City Workers." *Sun-Sentinel (Ft. Lauderdale, FL)* 21 Sept. 2002: 6A.

Jenkins, Colleen. "Too Young to Vote but Old Enough to Run an Election." *The Washington Post* 29 Aug. 2002: A20.

Keating, Dan. "Fla. Vote Uncovers a Problem: Overwhelmed Poll Workers." *The Washington Post* 14 Sept. 2002: A06.

Lipsky-Karasz, Daniel. "Harvard Study: Students Choose Community Service Over Politics." *Daily Princetonian* 9 Dec. 2002. *University Wire*. Lexis-Nexis. 4 Feb. 2003.

Olsen, Florence. "Researches from Caltech and MIT Track Improvements to Voting Process." *Chronicle of Higher Education* 13 Dec. 2002: 38+.

Schroeder, Cindy. "Need Ongoing for Election Workers." *The Cincinnati Enquirer* 29 Sept. 2002: 1B+.

Silva, Andrew. "Young Voters Care About Issues, But Turned Off By Partisanship." *San Bernardino Sun* 7 Nov. 2002. Lexis-Nexis. 4 Feb. 2003.

Eulogy to Princess Diana
Earl Charles Spencer, September 6, 1997

I stand before you today the representative of a family in grief, in a country in mourning before a world in shock. We are all united not only in our desire to pay our respects to Diana but rather in our need to do so. For such was her extraordinary appeal that the tens of millions of people taking part in this service all over the world via television and radio who never actually met her, feel that they too lost someone close to them in the early hours of Sunday morning. It is a more remarkable tribute to Diana than I can ever hope to offer her today.

Diana was the very essence of compassion, of duty, of style, of beauty. All over the world she was a symbol of selfless humanity. All over the world, a standard bearer for the rights of the truly downtrodden, a very British girl who transcended nationality. Someone with a natural nobility who was classless and who proved in the last year that she needed no royal title to continue to generate her particular brand of magic.

Today is our chance to say thank you for the way you brightened our lives, even though God granted you but half a life. We will all feel cheated always that you were taken from us so young and yet we must learn to be grateful that you came along at all. Only now that you are gone do we truly appreciate what we are now without and we want you to know that life without you is very, very difficult.

We have all despaired at our loss over the past week and only the strength of the message you gave us through your years of giving has afforded us the strength to move forward.

There is a temptation to rush to canonize your memory, there is no need to do so. You stand tall enough as a human being of unique qualities not to need to be seen as a saint. Indeed to sanctify your memory would be to miss out on the very core of your being, your wonderfully mischievous sense of humor with a laugh that bent you double.

Your joy for life transmitted where ever you took your smile and the sparkle in those unforgettable eyes. Your boundless energy which you could barely contain.

But your greatest gift was your intuition and it was a gift you used wisely. This is what underpinned all your other wonderful attributes and if we look to analyze what it was about you that had such a wide appeal we find it in your instinctive feel for what was really important in all our lives.

Without your God-given sensitivity we would be immersed in greater ignorance at the anguish of Aids and HIV sufferers, the plight of the homeless, the isolation of lepers, the random destruction of landmines.

Diana explained to me once that it was her innermost feelings of suffering that made it possible for her to connect with her constituency of the rejected.

And here we come to another truth about her. For all the status, the glamour, the applause, Diana remained throughout a very insecure person at heart, almost childlike in her desire to do good for others so she could release herself from deep feelings of unworthiness of which her eating disorders were merely a symptom.

The world sensed this part of her character and cherished her for her vulnerability whilst admiring her for her honesty.

The last time I saw Diana was on July 1, her birthday in London, when typically she was not taking time to celebrate her special day with friends but was guest of honor at a special charity fundraising evening. She sparkled of course, but I would rather cherish the days I spent with her in March when she came to visit me and my children in our home in South Africa. I am proud of the fact apart from when she was on display meeting President Mandela we managed to contrive to stop the ever-present paparazzi from getting a single picture of her - that meant a lot to her.

These were days I will always treasure. It was as if we had been transported back to our childhood when we spent such an enormous amount of time together - the two youngest in the family.

Fundamentally she had not changed at all from the big sister who mothered me as a baby, fought with me at school and endured those long train journeys between our parents' homes with me at weekends.

It is a tribute to her level-headedness and strength that despite the most bizarre-like life imaginable after her childhood, she remained intact, true to herself.

There is no doubt that she was looking for a new direction in her life at this time. She talked endlessly of getting away from England, mainly because of the treatment that she received at the hands of the newspapers. I don't think she ever understood why her genuinely good intentions were sneered at by the media, why there appeared to be a permanent quest on their behalf to bring her down. It is baffling.

My own and only explanation is that genuine goodness is threatening to those at the opposite end of the moral spectrum. It is a point to remember that of all the ironies about Diana, perhaps the greatest was this - a girl given the name of the ancient goddess of hunting was, in the end, the most hunted person of the modern age.

She would want us today to pledge ourselves to protecting her beloved boys William and Harry from a similar fate and I do this here Diana on your behalf. We will not allow them to suffer the anguish that used regularly to drive you to tearful despair.

And beyond that, on behalf of your mother and sisters, I pledge that we, your blood family, will do all we can to continue the imaginative way in which you were steering these two exceptional young men so that their souls are not simply immersed by duty and tradition but can sing openly as you planned.

We fully respect the heritage into which they have both been born and will always respect and encourage them in their royal role but we, like you, recognize the need for them to experience as many different aspects of life as possible to arm them spiritually and emotionally for the years ahead. I know you would have expected nothing less from us.

William and Harry, we all cared desperately for you today. We are all chewed up with the sadness at the loss of a woman who was not even our mother. How great your suffering is, we cannot even imagine.

I would like to end by thanking God for the small mercies he has shown us at this dreadful time. For taking Diana at her most beautiful and radiant and when she had joy in her private life. Above all we give thanks for the life of a woman I am so proud to be able to call my sister, the unique, the complex, the extraordinary and irreplaceable Diana whose beauty, both internal and external, will never be extinguished from our minds.

"Ain't I A Woman?"
Sojourner Truth, from the Women's Convention in Akron, Ohio, 1851

Well, children, where there is so much racket there must be something out of kilter. I think that 'twixt the Negroes of the South and the women at the North, all talking about rights, the white men will be in a fix pretty soon. But what's all this here talking about?

That man over there says that women need to be helped into carriages, and lifted over ditches, and to have the best place everywhere. Nobody ever helps me into carriages, or over mud-puddles, or gives me any best place! And ain't I a woman? Look at me! Look at my arm! I have ploughed and planted, and gathered into barns, and no man could head me! And ain't I a woman? I could work as much and eat as much as a man - when I could get it - and bear the lash as well! And ain't I a woman? I have borne thirteen children, and seen most all sold off to slavery, and when I cried out with my mother's grief, none but Jesus heard me! And ain't I a woman?

Then they talk about this thing in the head; what's this they call it? [member of audience whispers, "intellect"] That's it, honey. What's that got to do with women's rights or Negroes' rights? If my cup won't hold but a pint, and yours holds a quart, wouldn't you be mean not to let me have my little half measure full?

Then that little man in black there, he says women can't have as much rights as men, 'cause Christ wasn't a woman! Where did your Christ come from? Where did your Christ come from? From God and a woman! Man had nothing to do with Him.

If the first woman God ever made was strong enough to turn the world upside down all alone, these women together ought to be able to turn it back , and get it right side up again! And now they is asking to do it, the men better let them.

Obliged to you for hearing me, and now old Sojourner ain't got nothing more to say.

Resources for Finding Famous Speeches
(All working links at Press Time)

Representative American Speeches (Library Call#: PS 668 B3)

Contemporary American Speeches (Library Call#: PS 668 L5)

Vital Speeches (periodical; see also http://www.votd.com)

http://www.historychannel.com/speeches/index.html
History Channel Archive of Speeches (audio only)

http://www.pbs.org/greatspeeches/timeline/index.html
PBS' Great American Speeches

http://www.executive-speaker.com/spchlist.html
Links to speeches by major corporate executives

http://www.stkate.edu/library/internet/speeches.html
Links to famous speeches and quotations.

http://feminist.com/quotes.htm
Quotations by women

http://speeches.com/open.asp
For help writing ceremonial speeches

http://www.freedomvision.com/famousspeeches/home.htm
To hear several of Martin Luther King, jr. Speeches

http://douglass.speech.nwu.edu/
Douglass Archives of American Public Address - Lots of Speeches

http://gos.sbc.edu/
Gifts of Speech - Women's Voices from Around the World

http://curry.edschool.virginia.edu/curry/centers/multicultural/sites/hisspeeches.html
Historical Speeches Archives

Supplemental Materials

“Understanding the Chapter” Activity Answers

	#1	#2	#3	#4	#5
Chapter 1	F	F	F	F	T
Chapter 2	T	T	F	T	T
Chapter 3	T	F	T	F	T
Chapter 4	F	T	F	T	T
Chapter 5	T	F	F	F	F
Chapter 6	T	T	F	T	T
Chapter 7	F	T	T	T	F
Chapter 8	F	F	F	T	F
Chapter 9	F	F	F	T	T
Chapter 10	T	F	T	F	T
Chapter 11	F	T	F	T	F
Chapter 12	T	T	F	F	T
Chapter 13	F	F	T	T	F
Chapter 14	T	F	T	F	T
Chapter 15	F	F	F	F	F
Chapter 16	F	F	F	T	F
Chapter 17	F	F	T	T	F

Self-Evaluation Form: Ten Basic Steps

Name:

Specific Purpose of Speech:

Evaluate yourself in each of the following areas discussed in Chapter Three:

1. CARING

2. ORGANIZATION

3. STARTING & ENDING STRONG

4. LOOKING & FEELING GREAT

5. SHOWING YOUR PERSONALITY

6. *NOT* DROPPING THE BALL

7. CONTROLLING YOUR BODY

8. MAKING EYE CONTACT

9. CONTROLLING YOUR VOICE

10. AVOIDING REPETITIVE NON-WORDS

Self-Evaluation Form: Ten Basic Steps

Name:

Specific Purpose of Speech:

____

Evaluate yourself in each of the following areas discussed in Chapter Three:

1. CARING

2. ORGANIZATION

3. STARTING & ENDING STRONG

4. LOOKING & FEELING GREAT

5. SHOWING YOUR PERSONALITY

6. *NOT* DROPPING THE BALL

7. CONTROLLING YOUR BODY

8. MAKING EYE CONTACT

9. CONTROLLING YOUR VOICE

10. AVOIDING REPETITIVE NON-WORDS

Self-Evaluation Form: Informative Speech

Name:

Specific Purpose of Speech:

Evaluate yourself in each of the following areas:

1. TOPIC SELECTION

2. AUDIENCE ANALYSIS

3. CHOICE OF MAIN POINTS

4. INTRODUCTION & CONCLUSION

5. USE OF SUPPORTING MATERIALS

6. VISUAL AIDS (if used)

7. USE OF NOTES

8. EYE CONTACT

9. CONTROLLING YOUR VOICE AND BODY

10. OVERALL EFFECTIVENESS

Self-Evaluation Form: Persuasive Speech

Name:

Specific Purpose of Speech:

Evaluate yourself in each of the following areas:

1. TOPIC SELECTION

2. AUDIENCE ANALYSIS

3. CHOICE OF MAIN POINTS

4. INTRODUCTION & CONCLUSION

5. USE OF ETHOS

6. USE OF PATHOS

7. USE OF LOGOS

8. DELIVERY

9. HOW DO YOU THINK YOU PERSUADED YOUR AUDIENCE? (Explain.)

Grade-Your-Own-Outline Form

Before your instructor grades your outline, you can grade it!

Assign yourself points in the positive category for things you have done correctly, and take away points in the negative category for mistakes.

Attach this to the front of the outline you submit in class on the day of your speech!

ADD POINTS if you:

Have cited the minimum number of sources (20 points) __________

Have included a bibliography/works cited with all sources used (10) __________

Have a clearly stated general purpose at the top of the outline (5) __________

Have typed out your full introduction, including all four elements (15) __________

Have typed your full conclusion, including both required elements (15) __________

Have a balanced amount of information in each main point (10) __________

Have created a logical flow for all ideas in the outline (up to 25) __________

SUBTOTAL __________

SUBTRACT POINTS for:

An untyped outline (- 50 points) __________

Spelling errors (-2 each) __________

Grammatical errors (- 2 each) __________

Formatting errors (-2 each) __________

Inconsistent numbering/lettering (-3 each) __________

TOTAL POINTS (out of 100) I believe I have earned __________

Grade-Your-Own-Outline Form

Before your instructor grades your outline, you can grade it!

Assign yourself points in the positive category for things you have done correctly, and take away points in the negative category for mistakes.

Attach this to the front of the outline you submit in class on the day of your speech!

ADD POINTS if you:

Have cited the minimum number of sources (20 points) __________

Have included a bibliography/works cited with all sources used (10) __________

Have a clearly stated general purpose at the top of the outline (5) __________

Have typed out your full introduction, including all four elements (15) __________

Have typed your full conclusion, including both required elements (15) __________

Have a balanced amount of information in each main point (10) __________

Have created a logical flow for all ideas in the outline (up to 25) __________

SUBTOTAL __________

SUBTRACT POINTS for:

An untyped outline (- 50 points) __________

Spelling errors (-2 each) __________

Grammatical errors (- 2 each) __________

Formatting errors (-2 each) __________

Inconsistent numbering/lettering (-3 each) __________

TOTAL POINTS (out of 100) I believe I have earned __________

Source Citation Verbs

Verbs carry so much information. Beginners sometimes don't remember this and just repeat the phrase "according to" to introduce the sources of their information. For clarity and interest, try to use variety when selecting verbs:

adds, agrees, argued, ascertained, asserted, called for, claimed, confirmed, considered, contended, contests, debates, described, detected, determined, differs, discovered, discussed, disputes, encountered, established, estimated, explained, figured, found, further supports, held, hit, informed us that, learned, located, met, noted, noticed, observed, perceived, pleaded, pointed out that, pondered, proudly observed, reported, requested, rescued, retrieved, revealed, reviewed, said, suggested, summed it up best, surveyed, talked about, uncovered, unearthed, viewed, warned us that, wrote....

MLA Style Bibliographic Citation

All citations are **double spaced**. These have been single-spaced to save space.

Books

Typical Citation (see MLA Handbook, section 4.6)

Author. Title. City of publication: Publisher, publication date.

One Author

Herrera, Hayden. Frida: A Biography of Frida Kahlo. New York: Harper, 1993.

Four or More Authors

Belenky, Mary Field, et al. Women's Ways of Knowing. New York: Basic, 1986.

Selection in an Anthology

Gordon, Mary. "The Parable of the Cave." The Writer on Her Work. Ed. Janet Sternburg. New York: Norton, 1980. 27-32.

Article in a Reference Work

One Author

Johnson, Peder J. "Concept Learning." Encyclopedia of Education. 1971.

No Author

"Jonestown." Collier's Encyclopedia. 1996.

Periodicals

Typical Citation (see MLA Handbook, section 4.7)

Author. "Title of article." Title of Journal Volume.Issue (Date of publication): page numbers.

Journal is Paginated by Volume

Norris, Margot. "Narration under a Blindfold: Reading Joyce's 'Clay.'" PMLA 102 (1987): 206-15.

Journal is Paginated by Issue

Lofty, John. "The Politics at Modernism's Funeral." Canadian Journal of Political and Social Theory 6.3 (1987): 89-96.

Monthly Magazine

Weiss, Philip. "The Book Thief: A True Tale of Bibliomania." Harper's Jan. 1994: 37-56.

Newspaper

Markoff, John. "Cyberspace's Most Wanted: Hacker Eludes F.B.I. Pursuit." New York Times 4 July 1994, late ed.: A1+.

Video Recordings

Typical Citation (see MLA Handbook, section 4.8.3)

Title. Director. Medium. Distributor, Year of Release.

Citing the Contribution of a Particular Individual

Dionisi, Stefano, perf. Farinelli. Dir. Gerard Corbiau. Laser disc. Columbia TriStar Home Video, 1995.

Citing the Entire Recording

Unseen Life on Earth: an Introduction to Microbiology. Videocassette. Annenberg/CPB Project, 1999.

Electronic Resources

Typical Citation (see MLA Handbook, section 4.9)

Online Scholarly Project, Information Database, or Professional or Personal Site

Author of individual document. "Title of Document." Title of Site, Project or Database. Name of editor (if given). Electronic publication information, including version number (if given). Date of electronic publication or of latest update. Name of any sponsoring institution or organization. Date of access <Network address>.

Schriener, Olive. "Dreams." The Victorian Women Writers Project. Ed. Perry Willett. 25 March 2000. Indiana University. 27 March 2000 < http://www.indiana.edu/~letrs/vwwp/schreiner/dreams.html>.

Article in a Journal on the Web

Browning, Tonya. "Embedded Visuals: Student Design in Web Spaces." Kairos: A Journal for Teachers of Writing 2.1 (1997). 9 Oct. 1997 <http://english.ttu.edu/kairos/current/toc.html>.

Article in a Journal in an Online Database (see sections 4.9.2-4 and 4.9.7)

Dunn, Rita and Joseph Stevenson. "Teaching Diverse College Students to Study Within a Learning-Styles Prescription." College Student Journal 31.4 (1997): 3-7. MasterFILE Premier. Ebsco. 27 March 2000. Keyword: learning styles and college students.

Note: This citation is like a normal journal citation except that you add the name of the database (underlined), the database producer, the date you accessed the article, and the keyword(s) you used. Because URL's for online databases usually reflect scripting code and are not intuitive, this library suggests following Rule 4.9.7 for "no URL given."

COURTESY Deb Distante, Mt. San Antonio College Library

Searching the World Wide Web

Search Engines (Good)

Google (Recommended)
http://www.google.com

Alta Vista
http://www.altavista.com/

AllTheWeb
http://www.alltheweb.com/

HotBot
http://www.hotbot.com

Teoma
http://www.teoma.com/

WiseNut
http://www.wisenut.com

Directories of Searchable Databases – "Invisible Web" (Good)

The Invisible Web (Recommended)
http://www.invisibleweb.com

Direct Search
http://gwis2.circ.gwu.edu/~gprice/direct.htm

Inside the Web
http://www.searchiq.com/subjects/

Internets
http://www.internets.com

Search IQ
http://www.searchiq.com

Directories (Better)

Open Project (Recommended)
http://www.dmoz.org

About.com
http://www.about.com

Academic Info
http://www.academicinfo.net

Infomine
http://infomine.ucr.edu

The Internet Public Library
http://www.ipl.org/

Subject Guides or Gateways (Best)

Librarians' Index to the Internet
(Recommended)
http://www.lii.org/

The Argus Clearinghouse
http://www.clearinghouse.net/

Best Information on the Net
http://library.sau.edu/bestinfo/

BUBL Link
http://link.bubl.ac.uk

Digital Librarian
http://www.digital-librarian.com

WWW Virtual Library
http://vlib.org/Overview.html

MetaSearch Engines (Use with care)

Ixquick
http://www.ixquick.com

Dogpile
http://www.dogpile.com

MetaCrawler

http://www.metacrawler.com

ProFusion
http://www.profusion.com

SurfWax
http://www.surfwax.com

Vivisimo
http://www.vivisimo.com

Learn More

Finding Information on the Internet: A Tutorial
http://www.lib.berkeley.edu/TeachingLib/Guides/Internet/FindInfo.html

Internet Searching
http://www.library.uq.edu.au/internet/schhints.html

Search Engine Watch: News, Tips and More about Search Engines
http://searchenginewatch.com/

COURTESY Deb Distante, Mt. San Antonio College Library

Evaluating Websites

No person or group checks the information that is published on the Internet for accuracy or authority. ***You*** are responsible for evaluating the authority and accuracy of any information that you intend to use for research purposes. To do so, consider the following:

1. **What are the clues to "good" information?**
   - **Date** — is the date the information was written and/or last updated clearly marked?
   - **Author** — who is responsible for the information on the page? Does the page list professional credentials or experience which qualify that person/organization as an expert on the topic? What experience does the author have with the topic being discussed?
   - **Affiliations** — is the author identified with any group or organization, which might influence his viewpoint?
   - **Contact Information** — is there a way to contact the author (email, phone number, or postal address)?
   - **Background** — is the information presented verifiable in outside sources?

2. **Who is responsible for the information being presented?**
   - Is it from an individual or an organization?
   - What are the goals of the author in presenting this information?
   - Are the qualifications that allow the author to speak authoritatively on the topic listed?
   - Are the background and expertise of the individual/organization given?
   - If you have questions about any of these, email the author and ask.

3. **Where is the information coming from?**

- **Domain names** give basic information on where the data is originating. The domain name is the first piece of information after the http:// of an Internet address. For example, the domain name for Mt. SAC is www.mtsac.edu.
- **Extensions** are part of the domain name (such as .edu) and indicate the type of organization that is responsible for the information. Common extensions include:

.gov A U.S. government website. Governmental agencies publish most of their information online.
--Some level of editorial control over the content.

.edu A college or university website. The schools publish information, as do faculty, staff, and students.
--Limited editorial control of content.

.org An organizational website. Professional (American Medical Association) to political (NRA).
--Some editorial control of content, but must consider organizational goals.

.net An Internet service company. Internet service companies allow subscribers to publish websites.
--Only the author has editorial control of the content.

.com A commercial website. Commercial websites deserve the most scrutiny by researchers.
--Author has editorial control, which is intended to sell you something, whether a product or opinion.

4. **Did someone else consider this information to be acceptable?**
   - Was it reviewed or recommended in a professional journal?
   - Was it linked from another site whose authority and reliability you trust?

--Most **search engines** do not screen or evaluate the sites that they index.

--**Directories** and **pathfinders** are based on the selectivity of their creators.

5. **Can you write a 1-2 sentence explanation of why your Internet source is authoritative enough to include in your list of works cited?**

--Your audience will be looking at your works cited to determine how credible ***you*** are as an author.

COURTESY Deb Distante, Mt. San Antonio College Library

Topic Ideas: Informative Speaking

Automotive developments
Aeronautic developments
New surgical procedures
New medications & cures
Genetic discoveries
Space exploration and research
Criminology Developments
New security techniques
New trends in education
Unexplained phenomena
Military Developments/Technology
Unfamiliar cultures & traditions
Archaeological Discoveries

Good places to look for informative topics:

- Science Publications: *Science*, *Scientific American*, *Popular Mechanics*, *New Scientist*, *Discover*….
- Cultural/Anthropological Publications: *Smithsonian*, *National Geographic*
- Newspaper science and technology sections.
- Websites: beyond2000.com, stn2.com, popsci.com and technology sections of cnn.com, msnbc.com and abcnews.com, just to name a few.
- Your professors in other classes. Ask them about the latest developments in their fields!

Topic Ideas: Persuasive Speaking

Dangerous things...
Cell Phones/Eating & Driving
Malaria
Sleepy Doctors
Danger of Railway Crossings
Dangerous Playgrounds
Plastic Surgery Mishaps

Unjust things....
Genetic Discrimination
Online Cheating by College Students
Racial Profiling
HMO Mistreatment

Desperately needed things...
Run for office
Donate your organs
Minority Sports Coaches

Cruel things...
Elderly Abuse in Nursing Homes
Endangered Species Poaching

Controversial things...
Bilingual Education
School Vouchers
Term Limits
Gay Marriage

Good places to find persuasive topics:

- Opinion pages in newspapers
- Political publications: *New Republic, National Review, The Nation, Congressional Quarterly*
- Environmental/activist publications: *The Utne Reader*, *Sierra*, Amnesty International Updates
- Browse pending legislation. Try starting at: http://dir.yahoo.com/Government/Politics/

Impromptu Quotations

True humor springs not more from the head than from the heart; it is not contempt; its essence is love; it issues not in laughter, but in still smiles, which lie far deeper. (Thomas Carlyle)

'Tis the part of wise man to keep himself today for tomorrow and not venture all his eggs in one basket. (Miguel de Cervantes)

We have not journeyed all this way across the centuries, across the oceans, across the mountains, across the prairies, because we are made of sugar candy. (Winston Churchill)

A man's diary is a record in youth of his sentiments, in middle ages of his actions, in old age of his reflections.

Seeing is better than hearing. (African Proverb)

Long roads test the horse. Long dealings, the friend. (Chinese Proverb)

You say there is nothing to write about. Then write to me that there is nothing to write about. (Pliny the Younger)

As long as there are postmen, life will have zest. (William James)

Whatever is worth doing is worth doing well. (Earl of Chesterfield)

He who loses his temper is in the wrong. (French Proverb)

I am nothing, but truth is everything. (Abraham Lincoln)

A long tongue shortens life. (Persian Proverb)

Impromptu Quotations

Like all strong stuff, music is capable of becoming a principle o evil as well as of good. (Paul Rosenfeld)

A harbor, even if it is a little harbor, is a good thing, since adventures come into it as well as go out, and the life in it grows strong, because it takes something from the world and has something to give in return. (Sara Orne Jewett)

Questioning is not the mode of conversation among gentlemen. (Samuel Johnson')

He has left off reading altogether to the great improvement of his originality. (Charles Lamb)

Nothing prevents our being natural so much as the desire to appear so.
(La Rochefoucauld)

We would often be sorry if our wishes were gratified. (Aesop)

Service to others is the rent you pay for your room here on earth. (Muhammad Ali)

It's the good girls who keep diaries; the bad girls never have the time. (Tallulah Bankhead)

To be sure of hitting the target, shoot first, and call whatever you hit the target. (Ashleigh Brilliant)

Friendship is like money, easier made than kept. (Samuel Butler)

As long as people will accept crap, it will be financially profitable to dispense it. (Dick Cavett)

The important thing is not to stop questioning. (Albert Einstein)

An ounce of emotion is equal to a ton of facts. (John Junor)

Impromptu Quotations

Nothing is particularly hard if you divide it into small jobs. (Henry Ford)

You can't create a monster, then whine when it stomps on a few buildings. (Lisa Simpson)

Imagination is the one weapon in the war against reality. (Jules de Gaultier)

Doing a thing well is often a waste of time. (Robert Byrne)

When people are free to do as they please, they usually imitate each other. (Eric Hoffer)

The way I see it, if you want the rainbow, you gotta put up with the rain. (Dolly Parton)

If you believe everything you read, you better not read. (Japanese proverb)

The things you own end up owning you. (Tyler Durden "Fight Club")

Truth is not determined by majority vote. (Doug Gwyn)

If I am young, and right, what does my age matter? (Socrates)

It's not denial. I'm just selective about the reality I accept. (Calvin, Calvin&Hobbes)

My best friend is the one who brings out the best in me. (Henry Ford)

Never apologize for showing feeling. When you do so, you apologize for truth. (Benjamin Disraeli)

The only way to get rid of a temptation is to yield to it. (Oscar Wilde)

Impromptu Quotations

Never underestimate the power of stupid people in large groups. (Bumper Sticker)

What good is wearing your favorite rocket ship underpants if no one asks to see them? (Calvin, Calvin & Hobbes)

Without music, life is a journey through a desert. (Pat Conroy)

It's better to regret something you did then something you didn't do. (Red Hot Chili Peppers)

Be kind, for everyone you meet is fighting a harder battle. (Plato)

Tell a man that there are 400 billion stars and he'll believe you. Tell him a bench has wet paint and he has to touch it. (Unknown)

There's nothing so pathetic as an aging hipster. (Dr. Evil, "Austin Powers")

A life lived in fear is a life half lived. ("Strictly Ballroom")

Son, you tried and you failed. The lesson here is never try. (Homer Simpson)

You don't know what you've got 'til its gone. (Joni Mitchell)

The hand you hold is the hand that holds you down. (Everclear)

It's not where, but who you're with that really matters. (Dave Matthews Band)

Could I have been anyone other than me? (Dave Matthews Band)

Impromptu Quotations

Only two things are infinite: the universe and human stupidity, and I'm not sure about the former. (Albert Einstein)

I either want less corruption, or more chance to participate in it. (Ashleigh Brilliant)

No one ever listened himself out of a job. (Calvin Coolidge)

It's better to burn out than to fade away. (Neil Young)

It's easier to fight for one's principles than live up to them. (Alfred Adler)

The will to win is useless if you don't get paid for it. (Reggie Jackson)

Hope is a good breakfast, but a bad supper. (Francis Bacon)

Get busy living or get busy dying. (Andy Dufresne, "The Shawshank Redemption")

Pick battles big enough to matter, small enough to win. (Jonathan Kozol)

The 100% American is 99% idiot. (George Bernard Shaw)